JONATHAN SPENCE

Mao Zedong

A Penguin Life

A LIPPER/PENGUIN BOOK

PENGUIN BOOKS

Published by the Penguin Group

Penguin Group (USA) Inc., 375 Hudson Street, New York, New York 10014, U.S.A.

Penguin Group (Canada), 90 Eglinton Avenue East, Suite 700, Toronto,
Ontario, Canada M4P 2Y3 (a division of Pearson Penguin Canada Inc.)

Penguin Books Ltd, 80 Strand, London WC2R 0RL, England

Penguin Ireland, 25 St Stephen's Green, Dublin 2, Ireland (a division of Penguin Books Ltd)

Penguin Group (Australia), 250 Camberwell Road, Camberwell,
Victoria 3124, Australia (a division of Pearson Australia Group Pty Ltd)

Penguin Books India Pvt Ltd, 11 Community Centre, Panchsheel Park, New Delhi – 110 017, India

Penguin Group (NZ), cnr Airborne and Rosedale Roads, Albany,
Auckland 1310, New Zealand (a division of Pearson New Zealand Ltd)

Penguin Books (South Africa) (Pty) Ltd, 24 Sturdee Avenue, Rosebank, Johannesburg 2196, South Africa

Penguin Books Ltd, Registered Offices: 80 Strand, London WC2R 0RL, England

First published in the United States of America by Viking Penguin,
a member of Penguin Putnam Inc. 1999
Published in Penguin Books 2006

1 3 5 7 9 10 8 6 4 2

Grateful acknowledgment is made for permission to reprint excerpts from the following copyrighted works:
The Rise to Power of the Chinese Communist Party, edited by Tony Saich.
Reprinted by permission of M. E. Sharpe, Inc., Armonk, New York; *Mao's Road to
Power: Revolutionary Writings 1912–1949*, volumes I, II, III, edited by Stuart R. Schram.
Reprinted by permission of M. E. Sharpe, Inc., Armonk, New York; *Red Star Over China*
by Edgar Snow. Reprinted by permission of Grove/Atlantic, Inc.

Map illustration by James Sinclair

THE LIBRARY OF CONGRESS HAS CATALOGED THE HARDCOVER EDITION AS FOLLOWS:
Spence, Jonathan D.
Mao Zedong / Jonathan Spence.
p. cm. — (A Penguin life)
Includes bibliographical references.
ISBN 0-670-88669-6 (hc.)
ISBN 0 14 30.3772 2 (pbk.)
1. Mao Tse-tung, 1893–1976. 2. Heads of state—China Biography.
I. Title. II. Series: Penguin lives series.
DS778.M3S685 1999
951.05'092 — dc21
[B] 99-27739

Printed in the United States of America
Set in Electra • Designed by Francesca Belanger

Praise for *Mao Zedong* by Jonathan Spence

"Robust . . . this is an intelligent, adroitly presented, informative overview of the historical figure known for 'orchestrated' political purges and the 'unorchestrated' terrors of the Cultural Revolution. It provides a balanced view written with the sure hand of the knowledgeable historian."
—*Book*

"The task of bringing Mao to a large, non-specialist audience is one for which Spence is eminently well-suited. His lucidly written, compellingly narrated explorations of modern Chinese history have attracted a readership unmatched by that of any other academic China specialist. His study of Mao is short . . . his writing tight, his judgments restrained."
—*The Washington Post*

"An elegant account, at once sparse and robust." —*The Economist*

"Spence . . . compresses Mao's story into a read-on-a-plane format, a task he accomplishes without sacrificing his academic rigor."
—*The New York Times Book Review*

"An exceptionally successful contribution to Penguin's series of brief biographies."
—*The New Yorker*

"Simple but to the point. . . . Spence . . . draws upon his extensive knowledge of Chinese politics and culture to create an illuminating picture of Mao. . . . Superb."
—*Chicago Tribune*

"Jonathan Spence [is] a eloquent chronicler of Chinese history. . . . [A] brisk, elegant book. . . . Spence skillfully uses Mao's letters and poems to explore the Chinese leader's thinking and relationships." —*USA Today*

"There is no better person to write a general, readable account of Mao than Spence, an acclaimed Chinese historian and author of several biographies."
—*Library Journal* (starred review)

"Fluid and informative despite its brevity." —*Publishers Weekly*

"Spence is the best known and most talented historian of China writing in English today. . . . His *Mao Zedong* succeeds." —*Los Angeles Times*

For Annping

***

Kings ought never to be seen upon the stage. In the abstract, they are very disagreeable characters: it is only while living that they are "the best of kings.". . . Seen *as they were*, their power and their pretensions look monstrous and ridiculous.

William Hazlitt, *Characters of Shakespear's Plays*

FOREWORD

MAO'S BEGINNINGS were commonplace, his education episodic, his talents unexceptional: yet he possessed a relentless energy and a ruthless self-confidence that led him to become one of the world's most powerful rulers. He was one of the toughest and strangest in China's long tradition of formidable rulers who wielded extraordinary powers neither wisely nor well, and yet were able to silence effective criticism for years or even decades by the force of their own character and the strength of their acolytes and guards. Mao need not have done what he did, and it was he alone who ensured that his visions of social and economic change became hopelessly enmeshed with violence and fear. It was his rhetoric and his inflexible will that led to the mobilization of hundreds of millions of Chinese citizens, who—even when they wished to—could find no way to halt the cataract of energy swirling around them.

Those who endured Mao's worst abuses execrate his memory. Those who benefited from his policies and his dreams sometimes still revere him, or at least remember the forces that he generated with a kind of astonished awe. In the end it was really only physical decay and weakness that brought him down, even though his chosen policies had long been shown to be full of inconsistencies and what Mao himself termed "contradictions."

One goal of this book is to show how Mao was able to rise so high, and sustain his eccentric flight for quite so long. Context was naturally intrinsic to the drama, and the narrative tries to introduce the essential background that any reader needs to make sense of Mao's life. Historians in China and the West are slowly hauling Mao back down to earth, deflating the myths that sustained him, even as they often exclaim over the patience and deliberation with which Mao and his confidants constructed those same myths. We are learning more about Mao's relations with his family, friends, and confidential assistants; and Mao's own youthful writings, his poems, original drafts of several key speeches, and a good many surviving personal letters help us get some way into his mind. But many of the wilder flights of Mao's fancy, and the remarkable efforts he expended to attain them, take the historian out into a different zone, where the well-tried tools of exploration are of only limited help.

I have come to think of the enigmatic arena in which Mao seemed most at home as being that of order's opposite, the world of misrule. In the European Middle Ages it was customary for great households to choose a "Lord of Misrule." The person chosen was expected to preside over the revels that briefly reversed or parodied the conventional social and economic hierarchies. The most favored time for the lords' misrule was during the twelve days of Christmas, but they might preside, too, at other festivals or saints' days. When the brief reign of misrule was over, the customary order of things would be restored: the Lords of Misrule would go back to their menial occupations, while their social superiors resumed their wonted status.

In the European examples with which we are familiar, the

period of misrule was expected to be strictly limited, and the intention of the entire exercise was lighthearted. But sometimes the idea of Lord of Misrule would spill over from the realm of revel to the realm of politics. Milton wrote of the "loud misrule of Chaos," and the need to overcome it if the purpose of creation were to be realized. In the seventeenth century, some churchmen applied the Lord of Misrule label to Oliver Cromwell. The term also came to have sexual connotations, as in John Lyly's sixteenth-century play *Endymion*, when the hero declaims that "love is a Lorde of Misrule, and keepeth Christmas in my corps." Similar types of reversals could be found in many other European societies: in some, the apprentices took over from their guild masters for a reckless day or two, in others gender roles were reversed for a day as the women took over the tasks and airs normally associated only with men.

Chinese philosphers also loved the paradoxes of status reversed, the ways that wit or shame could deflate pretension and lead to sudden shafts of insight. Even if they did not specify the seasons, they knew the dizzying possibilities inherent in turning things upside down. To Chinese thinkers, the aspects of misrule were always embedded within the concept of order, for they were natural dialecticians, and understood that everything contains within itself the seeds of its own opposite.

It was Mao's terrible accomplishment to seize on such insights from earlier Chinese philosophers, combine them with elements drawn from Western socialist thought, and to use both in tandem to prolong the limited concept of misrule into a long-drawn-out adventure in upheaval. To Mao, the former lords and masters should never be allowed to return; he felt they were not his betters, and that society was liberated by their removal. He also thought the customary order of things should never be restored. There would be no Twelfth Night to end the Christmas season. The will of most people seemed frail to Mao, their courage to bear the pain of change pathetically limited. So Mao would achieve the impossible for his countrymen by doing their thinking for them. This Lord of Misrule was not a man who could be deflected by criticisms based on conventional premises. His own sense of omniscience had grown too strong for that.

ACKNOWLEDGMENTS

I OWE THE WARMEST THANKS to several people for their help with this book. Zhao Yilu was indefatigable in locating and translating recent Chinese sources on Mao and his family, and Argo Caminis made a broad computer review of recent Western sources. Professor Zhang Guangda read the first draft with care, and alerted me to several problems. Lorenz Luthi gave me copies of some important sources I had missed. Jesse Cohen's editorial suggestions were sharply on target. Betsy and Julie McCaulley, and Peggy Ryan, typed the drafts with their customary unflappable precision in the face of imminent deadlines. And Annping Chin, besides helping with Mao's poetry, kept me always alert to what his actions and visions had meant to others.

CONTENTS

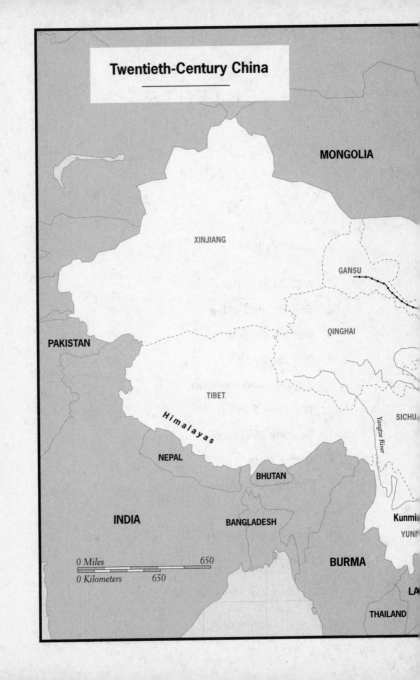

Twentieth-Century China

MONGOLIA

XINJIANG

GANSU

QINGHAI

PAKISTAN

TIBET

Himalayas

SICHU

Yangtze River

NEPAL

BHUTAN

INDIA

BANGLADESH

Kunmi

YUN

0 Miles   650

0 Kilometers   650

BURMA

LA

THAILAND

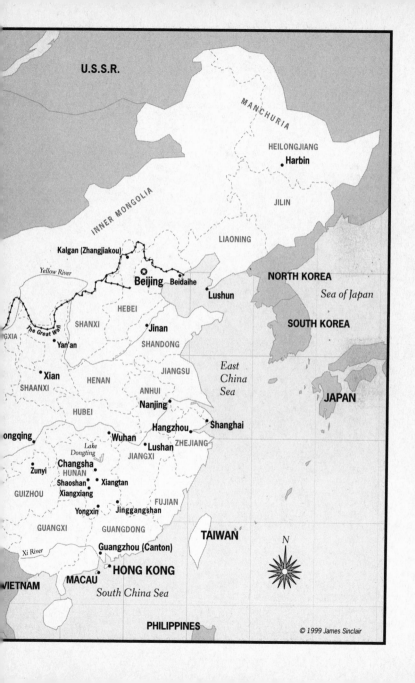

A Child of Hunan

MAO ZEDONG WAS BORN in late 1893, at a time when China was sliding into one of the bleakest and most humiliating decades in its long history. The Qing dynasty, which had ruled China with a firm hand for two hundred and fifty years, was falling apart, no longer understanding either how to exercise its own power or how to chart the country's course into the future. For over thirty years the Qing rulers had been trying to reorganize their land and naval forces, and to equip them with modern Western weapons, but in 1894 their proud new navy was obliterated by the Japanese in a short, bloody war that also brought heavy casualties to the Chinese ground forces. Victorious, the Japanese staked out major spheres of influence in southern Manchuria—once the ancestral home of the Qing rulers—and also annexed the Chinese island of Taiwan, transforming it into a Japanese colony. Before the century was out, the Germans had seized areas of north China, near the birthplace of China's ancient sage Confucius, the British had expanded the territory they dominated in central China, along the Yangtze River, and the French were pushing their influence into China's mountainous southwest. In 1898, an emperor with a broad view of the need for economic and institutional change was ousted in a palace coup only a hundred days after he began his reform program. And in 1900, as the old century ended, rebels in north China seized Beijing, and by killing scores of foreigners and thousands of Chinese Christian converts, brought upon their country an armed invasion of reprisal by a combined force of eight foreign nations.

These catastrophic political events occurred as other elements of Chinese society were feeling the stirrings of change. In some of China's large coastal cities like Shanghai and Canton, a class with many of the traits of the Western bourgeoisie began to emerge. Some members of this new Chinese middle class had been educated in missionary schools and had acquired a knowledge of Western science, religion, and political structures; others were exploring new aspects of business, discovering the effectiveness of advertising, distributing foreign goods inland, and experimenting with new forms of labor organization in their fledgling factories. This new middle class also began to subscribe to Chinese-language newspapers and journals that advocated political and social change, to use the postal and telegraph services newly installed by foreign companies, and to travel on China's rivers by steamer. But in a largely rural, inland province like Hunan, where Mao was born, such changes were barely felt. Only in the Hunan capital of Changsha might one have found a considerable clustering of self-styled reformers, and their eyes were turned more toward the far-off east coast cities than into the unchanging villages and farms that were spread all around them.

Mao Zedong was born in a sprawling courtyard house with a tiled roof in one of these farm villages, called Shaoshan, about thirty miles south and slightly west of Changsha. The exact date was December 26, 1893. He began to work on his parents' farm at the age of six, and after he was enrolled in the village primary school at the age of eight, he continued to do farm work in the early mornings and in the evenings. Their farm was small by Western standards, around three acres, but in that area of Hunan such a farm was considered a decent size, more than enough to support a family if well managed. As soon as his reading and writing skills were good enough Mao also began to help his father keep the family accounts, since his father had only two years of schooling. Mao stayed in primary school until some time in 1907, when he was thirteen and a bit; at that point he left school and began to work full time for his father, who had prospered in the meantime, buying at least another acre of land, hiring a paid laborer to help in the work, and expanding into bulk grain trade.

Mao's mother was born in an adjoining county, southwest of Shaoshan; although her birthplace was just the other side of a range of hills, in that highly localized rural society she grew up speaking a dialect that was quite distinct from her husband's. She bore seven children altogether—two daughters and five sons—but only three survived, all boys. Mao Zedong was the eldest of these three survivors, born when his mother was twenty-seven. The few records we have concerning his childhood and early adolescence suggest a timeless world, rooted in long-standing rural Chinese patterns of expectation and behavior. For months on end in his early childhood, Mao lived with his maternal grandparents and must have absorbed some of their gentler outlook on life—his father had served as a soldier in the provincial army before returning to the farm, and always had a quick temper and firm views. Family discussions often focused on his mother's Buddhism—she was a devout believer, while her husband was a skeptic. The young Mao was caught between the two, but sympathetic to his mother's point of view.

She had a kind of "impartial love," he said of her in his funeral eulogy (she died in 1919 at the age of fifty-three), "that extended to all, far or near, related or unrelated." He added that his mother "never lied or cheated. She was always neat and meticulous. Everything she took care of would be put in order. She was clear in thinking, adept in analyzing matters. Nothing was neglected, and nothing was misplaced."

Despite Mao's love for his mother, it was his father who laid out the lines of the boy's life: there would be five years of study in the Shaoshan village school, with a traditional teacher, in time-honored texts from the Confucian canon emphasizing filial behavior and introducing some aspects of early Chinese history from the first millennium B.C. There seems to have been no suggestion that Mao should do more than acquire basic literacy to help on the family farm; no hints, for example, that Mao might strive to pass the first level of the state examination system that would edge him toward the rural gentry life of those trained to work in the bureaucracy. In any case, if there had been such an intent, it would have vanished in 1905, just before Mao left school, when the court in Beijing announced the end of the exam system based on knowledge of Confucian classics. Mao's father encouraged his eldest son to be adept at calculation on the abacus; he had plans to apprentice the boy to work in a rice shop. If he valued his son's literacy for anything more than its teaching of filial behavior and practical bookkeeping, it was so that his son's knowledge of classical texts and use of some well-chosen quotations, produced at the right moment, "could help him in winning lawsuits."

Mao at thirteen, like any other healthy adolescent in China, was regarded as having moved from schoolboy status to adulthood, "doing the full labour of a man," in his own words; thus in 1907 his father arranged for Mao to marry a woman from the neighboring Luo clan. The Luos had land, some of the Luo sons were scholars, and the two families had close connections: the bride's grandmother was the sister of Mao Zedong's grandfather. The marriage took place in 1907 or 1908 when Mao was fourteen and she was eighteen. They were together for two or three years on the farm, until she died at age twenty-one. There is no record of any surviving children, and Mao did not discuss the marriage in later years.

Was it his young wife's death that broke Mao out of his apparently predestined circle of farm and family? Or was it already some deeper compulsion, some filtration into Shaoshan Village of knowledge about the dramas of the wider world? Mao Zedong traced it later to the impact of a book that a cousin sent to him at this time, a book that he added to his customary fare of historical novels about China's past. He had devoured such novels during and after school, going over the plots and characters again and again with his friends, until he "learned many of the stories almost by heart," and could exchange the tales with the old men in the village who prided themselves on their storytelling knowledge and abilities. This new book, so different from the others Mao was used to reading, was called *Words of Warning to an Affluent Age (Shengshi weiyan)*. Its author, Zheng Guanying, was a new kind of figure on the Chinese literary scene, a merchant who had worked with Western business firms in China, understood the foreigners' business techniques, and had dark forebodings about what might happen to China unless the foreigners were curbed. Zheng urged his compatriots to adjust to the modern world of rapid change before it was too late: by developing new communications systems such as railways and the telegraph, by industrializing, by creating a network of public libraries, and—most daringly of all—by introducing parliamentary government to China.

This book, Mao said later to an interviewer, "stimulated in me a desire to resume my studies." Though he did not have the money for any formal schooling, and his father would give him none, Mao left the farm in 1910 and found two tutors in the nearby county town of Xiangtan to work with him part-time, one an unemployed law student, and the other an elderly Chinese scholar. The law student widened Mao's horizons with current journal and newspaper articles, while the older scholar awakened in Mao a more profound interest in a range of classical texts than had ever been possible under the earlier pedantic village schoolteacher.

Among the eclectic mix of things that Mao read at this time—perhaps provided by that same cousin or by the unnamed student of law—was a pamphlet on "The Dismemberment of China," which covered such topics as Japan's colonization of Taiwan and Korea, the French conquests in Indochina, and the British dominance over Burma. Decades later, Mao still remembered the opening line, "Alas, China will be subjugated," and he attributed to the pamphlet the beginnings of his "political consciousness." Another incident, much closer to home, widened the range of his political feelings. A series of bad harvests in Hunan led to outbreaks of famine, and some of the desperate Hunanese formed a group under the slogan "Eat Rice Without Charge," and seized stores of rice from the wealthier farmers. Among the shipments they seized was one that Mao's father was sending to the county town of Xiangtan. Mao later recalled the ambiguity that this primal clash between family obligation and social desperation had aroused in him: he could not sympathize with his father, who continued to export rice from his farm in Shaoshan to the bigger county town markets, despite the local famine; nor would he condone the violence of those who seized the property of others.

Political news of a different kind filtered into Xiangtan, and to a new school in neighboring Xiangxiang township in which Mao enrolled late in 1910: tales of secret-society risings, of larger grain seizures and riots in the provincial capital of Changsha thirty miles to the north, of desperate villagers building mountain strongholds. Some of the incidents sharply revealed the extent of duplicity used by the authorities to regain or maintain their power: in Changsha, for example, rioters were first offered a general pardon if they would disperse, only to be later arrested and beheaded—"their heads displayed on poles as a warning to future 'rebels.'" In Mao's home village of Shaoshan, a group of villagers protested a legal verdict brought against them by their landlord; they were discredited, despite what Mao saw as the justness of their case, by the landlord's spreading of a totally fabricated rumor that they had sacrificed a child in order to gain their ends. Their leader, too, was caught and beheaded.

In the Xiangxiang school, centered in a bustling market town on major road and river routes, Mao found an eager group of volatile fellow students. The school had been brought to Mao's attention because it was "radical," and emphasized the "new knowledge" of the West. Convinced by neighbors that the school would increase Mao's earning power, his father agreed to his enrollment, and Mao was able to put down a deposit of fourteen hundred copper cash (around two U.S. dollars) to cover five months' room and board and the necessary study materials. Mao found himself despised for his rustic clothes, his lowly background, and for being an "outsider," even though he was from a neighboring county. Nevertheless, the school was a revelation to Mao. It offered courses in the natural sciences and in Western learning, as well as in the Chinese classics, and one of the teachers was a Chinese scholar who had studied in Japan, as many ambitious reformist youth were beginning to do. While in Japan, so as to appear "modern," this teacher had cut off his long queue of hair, a style that had been a distinguishing trait of Chinese men ever since the Manchus' conquest of China in the seventeenth century. Cutting off the queue was illegal in China, and Mao soon noticed that when the teacher taught, he wore a false queue braided to his own hair—another example of the odd anomalies of a China on the edge of transition.

This man taught music and English, and shared songs from Japan with his students. One of these was a hymn of triumph to the Japanese victory over the Russians in the war of 1904–1905. Japan's defeat of a Westernized power like Russia enchanted the students, who saw the possibility for a regeneration of their own country in the example of Japan's astonishingly swift race to modernization through industrialization and constitutional reform. "The nightingale dances / And the green fields are lovely in the spring," ran the lyrics of one of the songs that Mao remembered throughout his life; the students sang the words lustily, while the man with the false queue urged them on. Other teachers introduced Mao to a maze of new names and their accomplishments, to Napoleon and Catherine the Great, to Wellington and Gladstone, to Rousseau and Montesquieu, to Washington and Lincoln. At least one sentence stayed with Mao from a book he read that year called *Great Heroes of the World*: "After eight years of difficult war, Washington won victory and built up his nation."

These months in Xiangxiang township were the first time that Mao had been exposed to a wider world of contemporary events. It was only now, in 1910, two years after the event, that Mao heard of the death of the emperor in whose reign he had been born. And thanks to the same cousin who had lent him *Words of Warning*, Mao received in the mail the writings of two prominent reformers who had been exiled in the 1890s, when that same emperor had attempted an unsuccessful political reform movement. These two were the philosopher Kang Youwei and his disciple, the historian and pioneering journalist Liang Qichao. Both were fine classical scholars who became absorbed with the problems of China's future destiny. Kang's solution was to explore the ways that Confucius himself had sought to change the world, and to endeavor to establish in China a constitutional monarchy that might both keep the Qing dynasty securely on the throne and make China a more equal partner with the Western nations. Liang, more boldly, wrote of his feelings about the need of revolutionary change for China, citing the examples of the French revolutionaries; he also introduced Chinese readers to the complexities—and the hopeful model—of the Italian reunification and independence movement in the nineteenth century. In Mao's words from a quarter of a century later, "I read and re-read these until I knew them by heart. I worshipped Kang Youwei and Liang Qichao, and was very grateful to my cousin." But just as Mao had not been ready to approve the violence of those who seized his father's grain, so he was not yet ready for Liang's radicalism, and continued to consider himself a monarchist.

The new school's promise to teach the natural sciences had also been an attraction to Mao. But in a letter to a friend he confessed that he was "wearied by the burdensome details of science classes." If science was neglected, knowledge of China's own past continued to absorb Mao. Classical history was well taught at the school, and perhaps because as a good monarchist Mao "considered the Emperor as well as most officials to be honest, good and clever men," he continued to be "fascinated by accounts of the rulers of ancient China," and to read about them with sustained interest.

Good schools foster intellectual restlessness, and within a few months of leaving his home village and family farm for the county town of Xiangxiang, Mao was feeling the urge to go to the provincial capital of Changsha. Though Changsha was a large city, Mao did not have to fear being totally lost, for he had heard of a special middle school there for boys from his area. Armed with a reference letter from one of his Xiangxiang primary school teachers (he does not say if it was the Chinese scholar with the fake queue and the love of music), Mao walked the thirty-odd miles to Changsha. Half expecting to have his application rejected, he was admitted right away.

It was now 1911, and Mao was just seventeen. The Qing dynasty, already in such trouble when he was born, was by this time teetering on the edge of total collapse. Opposition to the Qing had found a new focus in the elected assemblies of local notables that had been founded in every province on orders from the court. The Qing rulers intended these assemblies to play a docile advisory role, but the assemblymen soon seized new prerogatives for themselves, expanded their base among the assertive new commercial and educated middle-class reformers, and began to push for the convening of a national parliament and the right to wield full legislative power. An exiled political radical from the Canton area, Sun Yat-sen, had also been patiently building up an underground revolutionary party in opposition to the Qing throne, and many of Sun's supporters were active in the same assemblies, or had friends who were members there. Sun's followers had also infiltrated the Qing armies, which were riddled with disaffection, despite the training in modern weaponry and discipline to which they were now being introduced. The Qing government itself, ruled by Manchu regents in the name of the new emperor, who was still only a boy of six, was reviled by many Chinese for its weakness in the face of the foreigners. The fact that foreign investors had gained financial control over much of China's emerging railroad system added fuel to this fire, and the Qing government's clumsy attempt to solve this problem by nationalizing the railways became a further volatile focus for provincial anger.

Mao found himself swept up in this excitement. As the capital city of Hunan province, Changsha was the seat of the Hunanese provincial assembly. Radical newspapers were widely available in the city, and Mao avidly bought and read them. In the spring of 1911, he and the other citizens of Changsha were galvanized by the news of a major uprising in Canton by Sun Yat-sen's supporters, and of the "seventy-two martyrs" who gave their lives in the name of freedom from the Qing yoke. Reading whatever he could find on Sun Yat-sen — Sun himself was still in exile at the time, shuttling among Japan, Southeast Asia, and the United States in search of funds and support — Mao became a convert, at least intellectually, to the revolutionary cause, though he still held on to his Xiangxiang primary school enthusiasms for Kang Youwei and Liang Qichao. Typical of his mood at this time, Mao recalled later, was a manifesto he posted on the wall of his school that spring, suggesting that Sun Yat-sen be made president of China, with Kang acting as premier and Liang as foreign affairs minister. He joined in student demonstrations in Changsha against the Qing, and clipped off his own queue of hair as a symbol of his new reformist self. When student friends of his whom he had thought to be revolutionary sympathizers expressed reluctance to cutting off their own queues, Mao and another friend took their shears and forcibly chopped them off.

The final Qing collapse began with a massive military mutiny in Wuhan, not far from Changsha, in early October 1911. Once rebels seized the city, other provinces rose in sympathy, often led by their provincial assemblies; Sun's Revolutionary Alliance members joined them, along with all those eager for change or frustrated by the government's incompetence. Mao heard a public address in his school from a member of the Revolutionary Alliance which so inspired him that he decided to leave at once for Wuhan to join the revolutionary army. Somewhat less than heroically, however, he delayed his departure while he hunted for waterproof shoes, having heard that Wuhan was a rainy city. Before he could locate the shoes, Changsha was occupied—almost without incident—by the revolutionary army forces led by two local leaders, and Mao could be no more than a spectator as the ripples of revolution spread through Hunan and out across the country. In February 1912, deserted by most of their former supporters, the Qing regents abdicated. China became a republic, led briefly by Sun Yat-sen, and then by one of the former Qing military strongmen who had also been interested in strengthening the state and recasting the form of the government.

The immediate lesson that Mao absorbed in these tumultuous events was the transient nature of fame and success. The two men who had done the most to bring the revolution to Changsha were Jiao Defeng and Chen Zuoxin. Jiao, from a wealthy Hunan landlord family, had studied briefly at a railway school in Japan before returning to China and founding his own revolutionary group with local secret-society support, which he named the "Forward Together Society." With some backup financial support from the Revolutionary Alliance, Jiao, still only twenty-five in 1911, managed to create a remarkable underground following among shopkeepers, farmers, craftsmen, coolies, and army personnel, whom he organized in a formidable array of front organizations. Chen had served in the Qing government's new army forces, where he rose to the rank of platoon commander, and became a close friend of Jiao's. The two men may have agreed with the basic republican goals of Sun Yat-sen, but they also had their own ideas about how the revolution in China should help the poor and the disadvantaged while at the same time increasing the power base of the affiliated secret societies.

Though they showed considerable courage and shrewdness in winning the city of Changsha to the revolutionary camp in October, neither Jiao nor Chen had a firm footing among the wealthy merchants and scholars who dominated the Changsha assembly. Accordingly, as soon as their radical goals became known, the two men were outmaneuvered and isolated by a number of local political leaders and military men, and they were killed in a sudden mutiny by the very troops they thought they were leading. As Mao succinctly described the events later in his life, Jiao and Chen "did not last long. They were not bad men, and had some revolutionary intentions, but they were poor and represented the interests of the oppressed. The landlords and merchants were dissatisfied with them. Not many days later, when I went to call on a friend, I saw their corpses lying in the street." It was Mao's first introduction to the realities of power politics.

The fates of Jiao and Chen seem to have given Mao pause.

He had missed his chance to join the first revolutionary army in Wuhan due to the speed of events—and to the elusive rain shoes. But when other students from Changsha schools hurried to enlist in a "student army" from the city to hasten the revolutionary cause, Mao was cautious. He did not exactly understand their motives, nor did he think the volunteer force was well managed. So instead he made the pragmatic decision to join the regular army—that is to say, the army once loyal to the Qing emperors, which had been won over to the republican cause by the rhetoric and skillful planning of Jiao and Chen. By a strange twist, therefore, Mao's commanding officers were now the people who had instigated the murders of both Jiao and Chen.

Mao did not see combat during his six months in the Republican army, but seems to have remained on garrison duty in Changsha. He did make some friends in his squad, two of whom were workers, one a miner and the other an ironsmith; they may have given him some new insights into the world of labor. If so, the conversations he had with them were doubtless sharpened by new reading that Mao was doing in his leisure time, in the pages of the *Xiang River Daily News*. This Hunan paper devoted considerable space to socialist theories—Mao said later this was the first time he encountered the word "socialism"—and also led him to read essays by one of the first socialist theorists and organizers in China. But when Mao tried to share this latest enthusiasm, in correspondence, with some of his former school friends, he found that only one of them showed any interest at all.

The members of his squad, however, looked up to him as an educated man, a new experience for Mao, who was now almost eighteen years old. They respected his "learning," and

Mao reciprocated by writing letters home for them. Perhaps this respect brought out a basic arrogance in Mao, even though it was not long since he had left the family farm, where he had been a laborer as well as his father's accountant. Mao now declined to go and fetch his own water from the springs or wells outside the city, as the soldiers were expected to do. As somebody who had been a student, Mao wrote later, he "could not condescend to carrying, and bought it from the water-pedlars." It was an odd kind of irony that the money he could have used to buy more socialist tracts was spent instead on buying water that he could easily have gotten for himself, but China was full of such twists of status. Army life, in any case, was not very fulfilling for Mao. Despite the antagonisms between different military and political leaders on the Republican side, the Qing dynasty itself had fallen with little more than a whimper, and China seemed set on a fair course toward the future. "Thinking the revolution was over," Mao recalled later, "I resigned from the army and decided to return to my books."

2

Self-Strengthening

IT WAS ONE THING for Mao to say he had to get back to his books. It was quite another to decide how to do it. For a few months in 1912, Mao simply browsed through the educational advertisements in the local newspapers, and (according to his later reminiscences) because of his gullibility and lack of experience, he was briefly convinced of the inestimable value of a whole range of special training schools, at least to the extent of sending in his dollar registration fee and in one case taking courses of a few weeks. The schools that caught his eye were for police training, legal work, commercial skills, and soap making. These new schools, with their promises of guaranteed careers for ambitious youth, were themselves reflections of the rapid changes that were sweeping China. Their claims were flamboyant because they were untried and unprovable, and, as Mao learned to his chagrin, some of them held their classes mainly in English, which he could not understand except for a few phrases remembered from his earlier primary school.

Perhaps on the rebound from all this new knowledge, Mao retreated in mid-1912 to the shelter of a more traditional middle school in Changsha, one with a predictable curriculum of Chinese learning. His teachers there encouraged him to explore China's own imperial past more deeply, believing that he had the "literary tendencies" to undertake serious study. One teacher led him through a collection of selected imperial edicts from the Qianlong emperor's reign in the eighteenth century, a period when China had been rich and prosperous, and had greatly expanded its borders. Others took him more deeply into earlier texts in classical Chinese than he had ever gone before, including the celebrated *Historical Records (Shiji)* by the second century B.C. historian Sima Qian, still regarded as China's greatest master of expository and narrative history.

Mao had almost certainly read some of these stories before, perhaps in simplified versions; it was at primary school that he began to delve deeply into the histories of early rulers, including the builders of the Qin dynasty, which after centuries of steady military expansion and administrative experimentation was finally in 221 B.C. able to draw all of known China together into a single centralized imperial state. One of Mao's middle school essays, dated June 1912, has been preserved and gives us an entry into his intellectual mindset at this time. It is an analysis of one of the Qin's first famous ministers, Lord Shang. Lord Shang was condemned by later Chinese scholars for his ruthlessness and deviousness, and for imposing savage and inflexible laws that terrified the people and reduced them to silence or to sycophancy. The historian Sima Qian said that Lord Shang was "endowed by heaven with a cruel and unscrupulous nature" and was a "man of little mercy." The eighteen-year-old Mao took a different tack. His point of entry into his own essay was an enigmatic paragraph in the center of Sima Qian's biography in which Lord Shang is presented as trying to convince the people of Qin to obey the new laws and take them seriously:

When the laws had been drawn up but not yet promulgated, Lord Shang was afraid people would not trust him. Therefore he set up a three-yard pole by the south gate of the capital market and announced that any member of the populace who could move it and set it up by the north gate would be given ten pieces of gold. The people were suspicious, and no one ventured to move the pole. Then Lord Shang announced, "Anyone who can move it will be given fifty gold pieces!" When one man moved the pole, he was promptly given fifty gold pieces, thus making clear that there was no deception. Then the laws were promulgated.

In his essay, Mao observed that when he read this passage he was drawn to "lament the foolishness of the people of our country." The Chinese people, now as in the past, were "mutually dependent and interconnected," so how could the people distrust their government? Lord Shang's laws "were good laws," Mao wrote firmly. Lord Shang himself was "one of the very first on the list" in the four-thousand-year-long record of those who had sought China's welfare. He defeated the states bordering Qin's territory, unified the Central Plain, preserved the people's wealth, and increased the prestige of the state and "made slaves of the indigent and idle, in order to put an end to waste." The fact that the people feared and distrusted him, so that he had to use the pole and the golden reward to convince them, was proof to the young Mao of "the stupidity of the people of our country," a stupidity that was ongoing and pervasive, and had led the people of China into a long period of "ignorance and darkness" that had brought the entire country "to the brink of destruction." The story of Lord Shang and the pole, Mao concluded, not only showed the innate stubbornness of the masses of the people—"at the beginning of anything out of the ordinary, the mass of the people always dislike it"—but constituted a shameful secret for the nation as a whole. If those in the Western nations or the "civilized" Eastern ones (Mao meant Japan) heard of it, they would "laugh uncontrollably so that they have to hold their stomachs, and make a derisive noise with their tongues."

That the derision of the foreigners should be seen as a potent factor to Mao is interesting in itself—by the first decade of the twentieth century the Chinese were circulating translations of various sharp critiques of their own country made by foreign missionary observers, as if to rub salt into their own wounds, and Mao had probably seen these in the newspapers he read so avidly. But more significant is Mao's self-confident acceptance of the necessity of Lord Shang's laws, despite the fact that those same laws had been seen by so many Chinese commentators across two millennia as ultimately destructive and self-defeating. The laws that Lord Shang had decreed included the following: all people in China would be grouped in units of five or ten households, linked in mutual surveillance and held mutually responsible under the law; those failing to report an offense of which they were aware should be cut in two at the waist; all families with more than two sons must declare the formation of a second household for tax purposes; people of all ages must "exert all their strength" in farming and weaving; profiteers and those "who became poor out of laziness" were to be arrested and made government slaves; social and economic status categories were to be sharply defined and backed by rules concerning clothing and ownership; and anyone giving shelter or lodging to strangers without proper credentials was to be prosecuted.

In the months after Mao wrote this essay, with its bleak view of China's ordinary people, China did in fact embark on the only broad-based political elections in its history. The elections were called under the rules of the new draft constitution promulgated in 1912, and a large number of political parties were formed and competed for seats in the new Chinese parliament— among them Sun Yat-sen's previously illegal and underground Revolutionary Alliance, now renamed the "Nationalist Party" (*Guomindang*). Candidates and voters in these elections had to be male, with certain educational or economic qualifications, and the elections were hard-fought, with the Nationalist Party winning the largest plurality but not an absolute majority. In a tragedy for China, Song Jiaoren, a close friend of Sun Yat-sen's and the architect of the Nationalist election victory, and who many had believed would be China's new premier, was assassinated in March 1913 as he waited in Shanghai to board the train to Beijing. The assassination may well have been ordered by China's acting president, the former Qing dynasty governor-general Yuan Shikai, but that was never proved. What was clear was that Yuan was bitterly hostile to the Nationalist Party, and that within a few months he had declared the party illegal and had driven most of its leaders, including Sun Yat-sen, once more into exile. For the next fourteen years, during the most important phase of Mao's schooling and young manhood, the Chinese republic became a sham, with the real power focused largely in the provinces and concentrated in the hands of local military leaders.

Mao commented on none of these crucial events of 1913, at least not in any sources that have survived. Instead he tells us that he spent this dramatic year of China's history wrapped up in an intensive period of private study in the Changsha public library. The establishment of such public libraries had been one of the priorities recommended by China's late Qing reformists, and now Mao was to reap the benefits. Though very short of money, and living in a noisy Changsha hostel for Xiangxiang natives, Mao established his own rigorous reading schedule during the library's open hours, pausing only at noon each day to buy and eat a lunch of two cakes of rice. According to his later memories, he concentrated his reading on "world geography and world history." As well as carefully scrutinizing world maps—the first he had seen—he plunged into his first serious study of Western political theory. Among the works that Mao recalls reading in translation during this time were Adam Smith's *The Wealth of Nations*, Darwin's *The Origin of Species*, and Herbert Spencer's *Logic*. Mao also mentions reading John Stuart Mill, Rousseau, and Montesquieu, and there is no reason to doubt him: by this time all the titles Mao mentions had been translated into Chinese and were available in China's better provincial libraries.

It must have been a solitary life, and one without clear purpose; certainly Mao's father thought so, and refused to send any more money unless Mao formally enrolled again in a school from which he might really graduate, and which might lead to gainful employment. Also, life in the Xiangxiang hostel grew intolerable, as fights flared regularly there between the students and the restless demobilized Xiangxiang soldiers and militia who used the same premises. When a group of soldiers tried to kill some of the students—Mao writes that he hid out in the toilet during this confrontation—he decided to leave. Once again, an advertisement caught his eye: it was for a school in Changsha called the "Hunan Provincial Fourth Normal School," and it offered free tuition along with cheap room and board. Urged on by two friends who asked him to write their application essays for them, and with a written promise of renewed support from his family if he was admitted, Mao applied in the fall of 1913. He and his friends were all accepted. "In reality, therefore, I was accepted three times," as Mao put it.

This was the school that drew things together for Mao; it gave him support and focus through teachers he both admired and respected, and a group of friends with whom to share life's travails and adventures. Mao was to stay there for five years. Even though he fretted under the restrictive regulations, especially the required courses in natural sciences and life-drawing (both of which he hated), he had outstanding teachers in classical Chinese and in the social sciences. The classical-language teacher made him restudy all he thought he knew about the early Chinese language, pointing out that Mao wrote like a "journalist," due to the pernicious stylistic influence of some of the reformers he had been reading so avidly. This teacher, whom the students nicknamed "Yuan the Big Beard," put Mao through an intensive course on the great Tang dynasty prose writers and poets of the eighth and ninth centuries, whom many considered the finest stylists in China's long history. Some fragmentary pages from Mao's surviving school notebooks, dated around December 1913, show the wide range of literary works that teacher Yuan discussed, and the detailed way that he led Mao (and the other students) through the variant classical pronunciations, the accurate translation of archaic economic and social terms, the exact identity of historical personages mentioned in the texts, and an analysis of the passages from various earlier Confucian classics chosen by Tang writers for inclusion in their own essays and poems.

Some of Mao's other notes show how carefully Yuan (or perhaps other teachers in the middle school) introduced and analyzed the work of poets from the mid-seventeenth century, who wrote in anguish at the victory of the Manchu conquerors over the once proud Ming dynasty. Such poems had complex racial and nationalist overtones in their contempt for foreign barbarians and their veneration of the long literary traditions of China's past. From such instructors Mao emerged with a decent familiarity with China's traditional culture, though not with the kind of encyclopedic sweep and depth of knowledge that would allow him to write or argue on an equal footing with those young men who had spent years working with scholars in their own private academies. And for the rest of his life Mao was interested in poetry and continued to write poems in the classical style even during the most strident periods of later revolutionary upheaval.

Strong though his literature teachers' impact may have been, it was Mao's social science teacher, Yang Changji, who was to have the deepest influence on Mao's intellectual life. As Mao recalled later, Yang "was an idealist, and a man of high moral character. He believed in his ethics very strongly and tried to imbue his students with the desire to become just, moral, virtuous men, useful in society." Yang was, by all accounts, a remarkable figure, and the fact that men of his background were now available to be the teachers of restless middle school students is one of the indices of how the intellectual world of China was shifting in the early twentieth century. A Changsha native born in 1870, Yang spent the years between 1902 and 1913 in a series of schools in Japan, Great Britain, and Germany. From these experiences Yang had developed his own broad-based system of ethics that combined the idealism of Kant and the theories of individual "self-realization" developed by British philosophers. The Changsha middle school position was Yang's first teaching job, and he led Mao and the other students through a rich series of ethical arguments, some of which he illustrated through selected passages drawn from the *Analects* of Confucius, and others by a careful reading of the German philosopher Friedrich Paulsen's *System of Ethics*, which had just been translated into Chinese. Yang explored the moral problems inherent in hedonism and utilitarianism, and in the evolutionary theories then becoming popular. At the same time he queried such deeply held Chinese beliefs as "Family priorities should come before national ones," and argued that intense family protection of the individual could in fact harm that individual's development of independence. Yang also encouraged Mao and other students to meet with such radical figures as the Japanese socialist Miyazaki Toten, who came to lecture at the Changsha normal school in March 1917.

Yang could not make Mao into a philosopher any more than Yuan could make him into a classical exegete, but Yang could and did introduce Mao to a global array of philosophical concepts, and gave him some of the analytical keys to continue his own investigations. By a lucky chance, Mao's original copy of Paulsen has been preserved, along with the marginal notes that Mao made during his senior year. The notations show him reading with close attention and occasionally expressing his own excitement in writing. Mao was especially intrigued to learn that moral philosophy always sprang from experience and that accordingly morality was different in different societies. From such a perspective, wrote Mao, "all our nation's two thousand years of scholarship may be said to be unthinking learning." Sometimes Mao's comments reflect his awareness of a different road opening up before him. Opposite Paulsen's comment that "all human beings without exception tend to stress self-interest over the interests of others," Mao wrote, "I really feel that this explanation is incomplete." And where Paulsen suggested that certain people were "devoid of feelings for the interests of others . . . [and] even take pleasure in the suffering of others," Mao exclaimed, "Except for those who are sick and crazy, there definitely are no such persons."

Many passages of Paulsen reminded Mao of Chinese philosophers or the early historical tales he had loved to read, just as others reminded Mao of something as local as the behavior of the lawless troops in Changsha, or as portentous as the fate of Republican China. Most moving, perhaps, are the moments when Mao read into Paulsen's words the deepest feelings of his own psyche. "This section is very well done," he noted next to Paulsen's powerful passage on the human wish to live "an historical life," one in which each person could "form and create, love and admire, obey and rule, fight and win, make poetry and dream, think and investigate." Sometimes Mao sighed over his new knowledge, as is seen in his handwritten comment on the pervasiveness of evil: "I once dreamed of everyone being equal in wisdom, and of the whole human race being made up of sages, so that all laws and rules could be discarded, but now I realize that such a realm cannot exist."

Yang not only wrote on ethics, he also wrote on physical culture and personal strength, and here his words touched another chord in Mao. Yang wrote that scholars in China were so physically frail that they were incapable of serving in the army, and hence military service was left to "scoundrels with little education." On the other hand, in Japan, as in the West, all kinds of sports from baseball and soccer to fencing and rowing were used to strengthen the citizenry, and in those countries outings to scenic spots were a basic part of life. Mao absorbed many of these ideas. He came to believe that exercise should be both violent and systematic, conducted in the nude if possible or in the lightest of clothes, and directed at strengthening the spirit as well as the body. By 1915 at the latest, Mao had begun to go on long tramps through the countryside with small groups of friends, staying with peasant families or in out-of-the-way mountain temples. He even posted notices around in Changsha, calling for "worthy men" to join him in these activities. After a day of hiking in the hills, the young men would swim in the Xiang River or one of its tributaries in the twilight; then they would sit on the riverbank and talk the hours away, discussing China's fate, the meaning of Western culture, the need for economic reform, and the best modes of social organization, before returning to their simple lodgings for a well-earned sleep. Mao never lost the love of swimming he developed during these years, and he often promoted it to his friends as the finest form of exercise.

It was surely because of Yang's help and encouragement that a lengthy essay Mao wrote on physical education, its spiritual and physical effects, and the best ways to exercise different parts of the body, was published in April 1917 in the prestigious Beijing monthly journal *New Youth*. This was the banner publication for new ideas in China, and was edited by a formidable group of scholars, many of whom were on the Beijing University faculty. At the same time, during 1917, Mao expanded his activities by forming a discussion society among his like-minded circle of students and friends, and by taking practice-teaching courses run by the middle school in the local community. In May, from the experience gained in the course, Mao and other students started a small school on their own, the "Workers' Evening School." The school offered instruction in basic math, reading, and writing, but also introductions to history, geography, "moral cultivation," and economics. Mao taught history. In April 1918, with the help of Yang Changji, a formally structured "New People's Study Society" met in Changsha. Mao was a founding member.

Throughout these years, Mao and other normal-school students were often invited to Yang's home. Yang had a daughter, Kaihui, born in 1901 just before her father left for his studies in Japan and Europe. She was raised until his return in 1913 by her mother, who sent her to a local school, at which Kaihui was the first female student. Later she transferred to an all-girls' school run by a teacher recently returned from Japan, who regaled the girls with tales of democratic revolutions. By 1911 or 1912 she was transferred to the Number One Changsha girls' school, where she stayed until her father's return. At this point, her father seems to have kept her at home so he could tutor her himself in both Chinese and English. Yang Changji was interested in problems of women's education and freedom for women, and in an article he wrote in 1915 for a radical friend's journal, he praised the free choice of marriage partners common in the West, and the equal rights that women enjoyed there. Yang felt that couples should marry late rather than early, and he denounced the practice of arranged marriages. He also criticized the prevalence of concubinage among wealthy Chinese. Mao must have met Kaihui—whom he was later to marry—fairly often on the visits to his teacher's home, though there is no evidence of any romantic attachment at this time.

At the meetings of the New People's Study Society, Mao was beginning to meet a number of other vivacious and politically radical woman, and by 1919 one of them, Tao Yi, became his girlfriend. She was three years younger than Mao, and also from Xiangtan county. Tao Yi graduated from the Changsha

Zhounan girls' normal school and was eager to go on for advanced study in Beijing, but she was too poor to do so. She made enough money to live on by a combination of school-teaching, cooking, tailoring, and crocheting, while she continued to study on her own. She was especially interested in psychology, theories of teaching, and the English language. As she told a group of friends in the New People's Study Society, she had "long thought about finding a partner for self-study, but several attempts [had] been unsuccessful." Though the two met often, and also corresponded, we know no details of their personal relations; but we do know that at this time there was a strange combination of emotions in the air for young men and women like Mao and Tao, a feverish sense of excitement that fused with a wish for chaste and enduring friendship built on a solid intellectual base of moral commitment. Even in the absence of any personal revelations, some sense of Mao's mental state as far as women were concerned can be gleaned from a passage of his 1918 commentary on the Paulsen text that he was then studying. When Mao came across this profoundly pessimistic sentence: "The natural man would . . . annihilate the whole universe merely for the sake of preserving himself," he erupted in protest. Mao's anguished marginal comment included the sentence: "For example, since I cannot forget the feeling I have toward the one I love, my will desires to save her and I will do everything possible to save her, to the point that if the situation is desperate I would rather die myself than let her die."

Mao completed his courses successfully at the middle school and graduated in June 1918. He was twenty-four. That same summer, his teacher Yang Changji received the offer of a professorship at Beijing University, the most prestigious institution of higher learning in China and the center of the intellectual excitement generated by *New Youth* and a host of other innovative magazines and journals. Not surprisingly, Yang accepted, left his home and job in Changsha, and traveled with his wife and daughter to Beijing. Mao initially stayed on in Changsha after graduation, but he felt aimless and listless. In a letter of August 11, 1918, to a former schoolmate, Mao wrote that he and his closest friends felt "our future is rather empty, and we have no definite plans." Some of them were getting local teaching jobs, while others were wondering whether to go to France on the newly announced work-study fellowships that would enable them to pay for their education by working in French factories. This program had been the brainchild of a group of prominent Chinese intellectuals. Some of these sponsors were self-professed anarchists living in Paris and studying the anarchist theories concerning the abolition of private property and restrictive personal bonds, and they believed in the ideal of mutual help as the way to solve social problems. Another sponsor of the program was Cai Yuanpei, the translator of the Paulsen edition that Mao had just been reading and the recently named chancellor of Beijing University.

The students chosen to go to France were to attend a training school first, either in Beijing or in Baoding city in north China, to prepare them linguistically and practically for the new life ahead. In a cryptic comment in the same August 1918 letter, Mao remarked, "I can raise the 200 *yuan* [Chinese dollars] for travel to Beijing and France, but the 100 *yuan* for travel to Baoding I cannot raise." He gave no explanation of why he could raise the larger sum but not the smaller one, but perhaps it was easier to get donations for foreign travel than for domestic journeys. A significant example of selective (or distorted) memory in Mao's later autobiographical reminiscences refers also to this same time. In the summer of 1936, Mao told his American interviewer, Edgar Snow: "In my last year in school my mother died, and more than ever I lost interest in returning home. I decided that summer to go to Beijing. Many students from Hunan were planning trips to France . . . [but] I did not want to go to Europe. I felt that I did not know enough about my own country, and that my time could be more profitably spent in China." But in fact Mao's mother was alive, though not well, all through 1918; she was having great difficulty swallowing, and it was also feared that she had ulcers. One other letter of Mao's has survived, also written in August 1918, to his "seventh and eighth maternal uncles"—that is, to his mother's brothers from the Wen clan. In this letter, Mao talks of his mother's illness and of his desire to find her a good doctor. He already had obtained a "special prescription" which he hoped would help her. In the meantime, Mao wrote casually that he was going to make a boat trip to Beijing with a few friends: "Sightseeing is the only aim of our trip, nothing else." There was no mention of money problems.

It was in this tangle of prevarications and half-truths, in August 1918, that Mao took leave of his ailing mother and for the first time in his life set foot outside his natal province of Hunan. When he arrived in Beijing he went to call on the Yangs, and asked the newly appointed Professor Yang to help him find a job.

Casting Around

PROFESSOR YANG found Mao a job as a clerical worker in the Beijing University library. A major part of Mao's duties was to register the names of all those who came into the library to read the magazines and newspapers. He was thus in the middle of everything, yet still somehow on the edge. The head of the library, Li Dazhao, only four years older than Mao, was already the center of an extraordinary galaxy of talented scholars. Li and five professors at Beijing University had formed a joint editorial board to run *New Youth* magazine. Their academic skills ranged easily across literary studies, philosophy, history, and music; several of them had studied in Japan, while others had advanced degrees from universities in the United States or Europe. The newly appointed Professor Yang shared their scholarly interests, and had published with them in other progressive journals even before *New Youth* was founded in 1915. By 1918, *New Youth* was publicly championing the cause of writing in the vernacular speech of China, rather than in the older classical norms, or the semi-simplified variants employed by the late Qing reformers. Already as a student in Changsha, Mao had switched his allegiance to the *New Youth* writers, but though he was now living in the midst of the *New Youth* ferment he was still nowhere near the inner circle, as the Yangs were.

New Youth magazine, along with the faculty and students of Beijing University, was at the literal and symbolic centers of the new China: the University buildings were just northeast of the Forbidden City, where the last emperor of the Manchu Qing dynasty, "Henry" Puyi, still lived with his eunuchs and retainers under the favorable clauses of the abdication agreement of 1912. Nearby were the buildings of the new parliament and the modern government ministries, and the foreign diplomatic quarter. A small public park had been formed outside the southern gate of the Forbidden City, at Tiananmen, the Gate of Heavenly Peace, an area once home to Qing government officials. Students and townspeople gathered there under the trees to talk and debate the political issues of the day, which were legion: the president of the Republic, Yuan Shikai, had died in 1916, after a disastrous attempt to establish himself as the emperor of a new dynasty; in 1917 a pro-Manchu militarist attempted to restore the emperor Puyi but was foiled by an alliance of rival generals; the same year, Sun Yat-sen returned from exile in Japan to form a separatist regime in southeastern China, in Canton; also in 1917, the new premier of the Republic made a deal with the British and the French to send over a hundred thousand Chinese coolie laborers to the World War I battlefields in Europe to help unload and transport war materials, maintain the base camps, and remove the corpses from the battlefields. The payoff to China was meant to be recovery of the territory previously ceded to Germany in the late Qing, but through corruption by the Chinese politicians and special deals with the Western powers, most of these hoped-for gains had already been mortgaged to Japan. The parliament of China, with the Guomindang Nationalists still excluded, was a shadowy forum with little real power, where all votes were regarded as being for sale.

In the library, Mao saw many of the influential figures of the new intellectual elite, and his mind must have been filled with questions. As a contributor and devout reader of *New Youth*, he would have seen Li Dazhao's essay describing the cycles of birth, decay, and regeneration within national histories, as well as Li's essay on "The Victory of Bolshevism" for the October 1918 issue. Here Li did what few if any in China had yet done, he hailed the revolutionary new order of the Soviet Union, after the Bolshevik Revolution of 1917, and briefly discussed the Marxist social and economic theories on which it was based. That same year Li also started a group that met at intervals to discuss revolutionary theory, which he named the "Research Society for the Study of Marxism." Such glimmers of interest in Marxism still had to compete with numerous other intellectual explorations in *New Youth* and within Beijing University at the same time. Li's colleague, the philosopher and literary critic Hu Shi, for instance, published the first lengthy analysis of Ibsen and feminist theory to appear in China, following it up with a lengthy essay on the emancipation of American women. (Hu, only two years older than Mao, already had a bachelor's degree from Cornell and had been a graduate student at Columbia). Elsewhere in *New Youth*, and in dozens of other new magazines in Beijing, Shanghai, and smaller provincial cities, students and their teachers were exploring themes ranging from Bertrand Russell's mathematical logic and Einstein's ideas of relativity to Margaret Sanger's birth-control advice and Rabindranath Tagore's pacifist communalism. It was an unusually bewildering time to be young.

It was at this time, according to Mao's later candid comment to Edgar Snow, that he "fell in love with Yang Kaihui," the daughter of his former ethics teacher. She was just eighteen, and Mao was twenty-five. Mao recalled those winter months of early 1919 with unusual lyricism, perhaps because he still saw it with the aid of her eyes. It was, he said, "in the parks and the old palace grounds" of Beijing that he saw the willows bowed down by "the ice crystals hanging from them" and watched "the white plum blossoms flower while the ice still held solid over the North Lake." Love might have been blossoming, but he had almost no money and Beijing was very expensive. Mao was used to the educational world of Changsha, where in five years of normal school he had spent a total of only 160 Chinese dollars. Now in Beijing, with a salary of eight dollars a month, and no hostel for Xiangxiang natives, Mao lived off a narrow lane in a poor district called "Three Eyes Well," sharing three small rooms with seven other fellow students from Hunan. And he found the Beijing intellectuals aloof and self-important: "I tried to begin conversations with them on political and cultural subjects, but they were very busy men. They had no time to listen to an assistant librarian speaking southern dialect." Mao did join at least two study groups, one on philosophy and the other on journalism, and sat in on some classes. It is possible, too, that Professor Yang, with his belief in late marriage, found Mao's courtship of his only daughter premature. For whatever reasons, Mao was not at ease in Beijing, and when he received a letter from home telling him that his mother was seriously ill, he decided to leave. Borrowing money from friends, on March 12 he took a train to Shanghai, arriving on the fourteenth. There Mao lingered for twenty days while he said farewell to a number of his friends and former classmates who were setting off for France; after they had sailed, he borrowed more money and made his way back across the country to Changsha, reaching home on April 6.

To what extent was Mao the prodigal son returned? He told his family members that he had been "a staff member of Beijing University," which left unclear exactly what he had done in the capital. But for now, with both his ill mother and his own future to think of, Mao took a job teaching history in a Changsha primary and middle school (it also had a teacher-training department) known as the "Study School." He stayed there until December 1919. As well as teaching, Mao embarked on a burst of writing, clearly stimulated by his stay in the volatile intellectual world of Beijing. In his earlier school days, his classical literature teacher Yuan had mocked him for being a journalist overinfluenced by Liang Qichao. Forced to follow the great events of the May 4 students' demonstrations in Beijing at a distance—the demonstrations, directed against the corrupt Beijing regime that had betrayed China to Japan, and against United States support for Japan's position, led to the designation of this whole period of intellectual ferment as the "May Fourth Movement"—Mao decided to keep the students and citizens of Changsha up-to-date with the news. He did this through a journal he edited, the *Xiang River Review*, which he also wrote almost entirely himself, producing four issues at weekly intervals between July 14 and August 4, until the local warlord closed the magazine down.

In Mao's "manifesto" for the new journal, dated July 14, 1919, he gave what we may assume to be an accurate summary of his political views that summer. It was an emotional voice, deeply influenced by the rhetoric of Li Dazhao, that attempted an overarching view of human destiny and world history. A movement for the "liberation of mankind" was under way, wrote Mao, and all old prejudices must be questioned. All old fears must be jettisoned too—fear of heaven, spirits, the dead, the bureaucrats, the warlords, the capitalists. The West had followed a route of "emancipation" that led through the Renaissance and the Reformation to the formation of representative governments with universal suffrage and the League of Nations. "Democracy," however one chose to translate it into Chinese—Mao offered his readers four variants of acceptable Chinese renderings—was the central name for the movement against oppression in all its forms: religious, literary, political, social, educational, economic, and intellectual. But in fighting oppression one should not use the tools of oppression—that would be self-defeating. Instead, one should "accept the fact that the oppressors are people, are human beings like ourselves," and that their oppressive acts are not so much willed by them, but are more like "an infection or hereditary disease passed on to them from the old society and old thought." China was facing a revolution that cried out for bread, for freedom, and for equality; there was no need for a "revolution of bombs or a revolution of blood," Mao wrote. Japan was the worst of the international oppressors, and he felt it should be dealt with by means of economic boycotts and student and worker strikes. To achieve this, the "popular masses" of China—"simple untutored folk"—should be educated and their minds broadened beyond the shores of their own Xiang River to grasp "the great world tides rolling in. . . . Those who ride with the current will live; those who go against it will die." As part of his own contribution to this program, Mao wrote twenty-six articles on Chinese and world history for the first issue, and printed two thousand copies, which sold out in a day.

Increasing the print run to five thousand for the subsequent issues, Mao continued to write short essays and also a lengthy manifesto entitled "The Great Union of the Popular Masses," which took up the majority of issues two through four. In this essay Mao laid forth a whole range of possible union organizations to give strength to those waging the struggle ahead—not just unions of workers, farmers, and students, but also of women, primary school teachers, policemen, and rickshaw pullers. To give a sense of the continuity of the struggle, Mao also published a detailed history of the various organizations of students in Hunan since the late Qing period, not neglecting to mention the role of major athletic meets as opportunities for student solidarity in the face of the oppressors. For the fifth issue, Mao promised his five thousand readers a detailed account of the "Hunan student army."

In all these writings, Mao was either implicitly or overtly criticizing the ruling militarist in Hunan, General Zhang Jingyao, who seemed to represent everything against which Mao was now beginning to rebel. Like others in this period, Zhang had acquired his early knowledge of soldiering as a bandit, before transferring into a military academy and, after graduation, joining the coterie of a powerful northern Chinese politician. Through personal contacts and his control of a sizable body of troops he was appointed military governor of Hunan in 1918, after a savage war in which tens of thousands of Hunanese were killed, and even more homes and businesses were destroyed. Zhang brought with him into Hunan as senior administrators his three brothers, all as ruthless and corrupt as he was. It is not surprising that when Zhang heard of Mao's fifth journal issue, with its provocative subject matter, he ordered all copies confiscated and destroyed. Unfazed, Mao got himself appointed as the editor of another journal, the *New Hunan*, for which he penned a new but far briefer manifesto. This journal, he declared, would have four guiding principles: to criticize society, to reform thought, to introduce new learning, and to discuss problems. All power or "authority"—Mao printed this word in English, which he was struggling to learn at this time—

that might endeavor to silence them would be ignored. Mao might have believed that this journal would receive a measure of protection because it was the organ of the Yale-in-China association in Changsha (the American university's offshoot in China), founded after the Boxer Uprisings of 1900 to bring Western medical education to China. If so, he was mistaken. This journal, too, was suppressed after one issue, by the same General Zhang.

Blocked from this new avenue, Mao became a regular contributor to Changsha's largest newspaper, the *Dagongbao*. It was for this paper that he wrote a series of nine articles on the suicide of a local Changsha woman named Zhao Wuzhen, which attracted wide attention. Zhao had killed herself inside her enclosed bridal sedan chair, as she was being taken to an arranged marriage that she bitterly opposed. Mao used the opportunity to develop the ideas he had absorbed from Yang Changji, and other writers for *New Youth*, about the need to end old marriage customs, abolish matchmakers and their endless "cheap tricks," and inaugurate an era of freedom of choice and economic opportunities for women in the new China.

During this period of the summer and fall of 1919, Mao continued to work on organizing the Hunan "United Students' Association," and in December he organized a widely supported student strike of thirteen thousand middle school students against Zhang Jingyao, who had further alienated all teachers and students by slashing the Hunan educational budget, cutting teachers' merit raises, blocking teachers' salaries, beating up those who protested, and billeting his unruly troops inside school buildings. All this was in addition to Zhang's troops' ongoing record of extraordinary cruelty to farmers' families in the countryside, his seizure of banks' assets, and his proven record of massive opium smuggling and the illegal selling of lead-mining rights to German and American businessmen. Zhang's harsh repression of the student strike led Mao to consider his own future options with renewed care. Furthermore, Mao's mother died that fall, on October 5, and, presiding at the funeral on October 8, he gave a loving oration in her memory. He was still unmarried and had become something of a marked figure in Changsha, as well as a definite thorn in the side of the dangerous General Zhang. So in December, Mao traveled once again to Beijing to see the Yangs, to attempt to deepen his contacts with Li Dazhao and other writers he admired, and to seek support for a national campaign to oust the corrupt general Zhang from Hunan Province.

Mao arrived in Beijing to find Professor Yang Changji desperately ill. A gastric illness the previous summer had somehow led to massive swelling of his body and to collapse of his digestive system. Convalescence in the scenic western hills, and specialized care in the Beijing German hospital, had alike been unavailing. Yang's colleagues ascribed the illness to overwork at Beijing University, where he was teaching a full load besides translating two books on Western ethics and writing educational surveys. Yang died at dawn on January 17, 1920, and on January 22, just a few months after giving the eulogy at his own mother's funeral, Mao became the cosignatory of the funeral eulogy for his most influential teacher. One day later, on January 23, Mao's father died at his home in Shaoshan.

Mao, however, stayed on in Beijing. There must have been family matters to attend to back in Hunan, but there was a lot to do in Beijing. There were the Yangs, mother and daughter, to see to. Most important to Mao's political future was Li Dazhao, whom he now got to know better, for both were mourning the loss of a mutual friend. Li now had organized a more formal Marxist Study Society in Beijing, and a translation of the *Communist Manifesto* was under way (some of it already completed, for Mao to see) along with more technical works like Karl Kautsky's *Economic Doctrines of Karl Marx*. Yet if Mao was now getting a more specific knowledge of Marxist-socialist theories, he remained very eclectic in his own mind—his surviving letters to friends from this time show him dreaming of a wide range of options, including a work-study school in the verdant Yuelu hills outside Changsha, a dream he had harbored since 1918. The students and teachers would learn and work at farming in all its aspects—from tending vegetables and flowers to raising rice and cotton, growing mulberry trees, and breeding fish and poultry. (Mao noted that such work would be regarded as "sacred," but if the "rough work" was too hard for the students, then "hired hands should be employed to assist them.") If farming proved impractical, an alternate approach would be to found a "Self-Study University" in which the teachers and students "would practice a Communist life." Income for this project would be derived from teaching, publishing essays and articles, and editing books, and expenses would be cut by having the community do its own cooking and laundry. All income would be held in common, for this would also be a "work-study mutual aid society." Intellectual focus would come from an "Academic Symposium," meeting two or three times a week. After two or three years of such training the students and teachers might be able to set off for Russia, which Mao was now defining as "the number one civilized country in the world."

Mao, in other words, was restless. As he wrote in March 1920 to a friend whose own mother had also just died, there was now a whole category of "people like us, who are always away from home and are thereby unable to take care of our parents." In a letter to his girlfriend, Tao Yi, who was teaching in Changsha but hoping to come to Beijing, Mao repeated that he would like to go to Russia. To make that dream a reality, once things were peaceful again in Hunan he would form a "Free Study Society" in Changsha, hoping "to master the outline of all fields of study, ancient and modern, Chinese and foreign." Mao added, "Then I will form a work-study team to go to Russia." He was confident, he told Tao Yi, that women going to Russia would "be particularly welcomed by the Russian women comrades." He had been "consulting" Li Dazhao on this and other matters, he added. The reasons for *not* going abroad, however, were also considerable. Since one could read translations so much faster than the foreign-language originals, one could learn more and faster in China. "Oriental civilization," wrote Mao, "constitutes one half of world civilization. Furthermore, Eastern civilization can be said to be Chinese civilization." So why go anywhere?

When Mao did leave Beijing at last, on April 11, it was for Shanghai. This time he took twenty-five days for the trip, stopping off on the way at the north China sacred mountain of Taishan and at Confucius's hometown of Qufu. In Shanghai he stayed with three other activists from the movement to expel Governor Zhang from Hunan. In early June, Mao was considering learning Russian—all three of his housemates wanted to go to Russia—and trying, he told a friend, "to find a Russian with whom to study the Russian language," but he had trouble finding one. Mao was also trying to learn English, "reading one short lesson from the simplest primer every day." Self-study was going to be his rule from now on: "I have always had an intense hatred for school, so I have decided never to go to school again."

As to philosophy, he was concentrating on Bergson, Russell, and Dewey. Mao also found the time and opportunity to meet with Chen Duxiu, one of the key radical faculty leaders of the May Fourth Movement, and the sponsor of the full translation of the *Communist Manifesto*, which was just being completed.

Fate solved Mao's indecisiveness with startling suddenness when a rival coalition of political and military leaders unexpectedly attacked Changsha and drove out the hated General Zhang. It turned out that Mao had hitched his wagon to the right star after all: one of his former teachers with the requisite political contacts was named director of the Changsha normal school, and used his new influence to appoint Mao director of the attached primary school. On July 7, 1920, Mao was back in Changsha with a respected career opened up in front of him, and he moved swiftly to assert his presence. In just over three weeks after his return, on July 31, 1920, Mao announced to the local newspapers the formation of yet another new venture, one that would draw together at least some of his dreams of the previous years. It was to be called the "Cultural Book Society."

Mao's announcement started banteringly: How would one expect to find "new culture" in Hunan? Few of the thirty million Hunanese had received any schooling. Of those who had, only a few were "functionally literate." And of the literate, how many knew what the new culture was? New culture was not just a matter of "having read or heard a few new terms." Indeed most of the world, not just Hunan, had no knowledge of new culture. At this point Mao boldly inserted a phrase that showed the definite orientation of his thought: "A tiny blossom of New Culture has appeared in Russia, on the shores of the Arctic Ocean." The Cultural Book Society would try to ensure that this blossom would flower in Hunan. A bookstore would start the process, but a research wing, along with editorial and printing facilities, would soon be added. Through Chinese and foreign books, the new culture would reach across Hunan. The conclusion to the announcement had a special slant, emphasizing that this was no conventional capitalist enterprise. It had been founded "by a few of us who understand and trust each other completely." None of the money that had been invested would be withdrawn by the investors. There would be no dividends. Joint ownership would be perpetual. No one would take a penny of profit if it succeeded; "If it fails, and not a penny is left from the venture, we will not blame one another. We will be content to know that on this earth, in the city of Changsha, there was once a 'collectively owned' Book Society."

Mao listed himself among the original investors when the Cultural Book Society issued its first report on October 22, 1920. So how had he raised the money for the shop? Had Mao received a sizable inheritance, in the form of land and the cash profits from his father's trading ventures? This would explain why Mao in 1920 apparently had none of the financial problems living in Beijing and traveling by train to Shanghai that had plagued him in 1919. And even though Mao drew no wages as manager of the bookshop, he had his salary as director of the primary school. Furthermore, Mao began to push the cause of Hunan independence with extraordinary energy after he returned to Changsha in July, and this was a cause dear to the heart of many wealthy businessmen and to the new governor of the province, Tan Yankai. Mao's backers certainly covered a wide spectrum: as well as local business leaders, Mao listed the Beijing Marxist Li Dazhao as one of the "credit references" who persuaded the local book and magazine distributors to waive their customary security deposits.

Then there was the curious fact that the store run by the Cultural Book Society itself was not located in a Chinese-owned site in Changsha, as the board had apparently planned, nor in the city education building as some had suggested, but was rented from the Hunan-Yale medical school, the offshoot of the original Yale-in-China mission in the city. The guarantor of this lease—which was publicly announced in the director's report—was a well-known Hunanese cultural and educational leader, who also invested in the venture (as did Mao's friend Tao Yi, who put up ten silver dollars, although she was always so desperately short of money). Certainly the business was well-run, despite its unusual character and structure. According to the figures prepared by Mao Zedong—it was not for nothing, his father's insistence that he learn accounting—income from sales for the first announced financial period was 136 Chinese dollars, while expenses, including the rent and start-up equipment, were only 101 Chinese dollars. With a surplus of 35 dollars from its sales of New Youth, and authors such as Bertrand Russell, Hu Shi, and Kropotkin, the Cultural Book Society's store was turning a profit of more than 30 percent.

Mao seemed to have found a new niche as a businessman, bookseller, and school principal, and it was time to think of the future. Certainly Tao Yi had been generous, and was an independent spirit. But Yang Kaihui had returned to Changsha after her father's death, and also was regarded as a bold pioneer in women's educational circles, with her own excellent range of contacts. At her father's funeral back in January there had been a public appeal—cosigned by Mao Zedong—for funds to help Yang Kaihui and her younger brother, who it was alleged had been left with no "means of support." But in fact her father had owned some land in or near Changsha, and the appeal stipulated that the money raised for the children "could either constitute savings or be used as capital for a business." So now neither Mao nor his teacher's daughter was destitute, and they obviously had a great deal in common. In late 1920, Mao Zedong and Yang Kaihui began living together.

4

Into the Party

THE FIRST TIME that Mao in his own writings discussed the Russian revolutionary leader Lenin at any length was in an article of September 1920. The context, rather surprisingly, was Hunanese independence, for which Mao had become a forceful spokesman. In his essay, Mao argued that China's apparent size and strength had always been deceptive: when it was examined more closely, one could see that China had been "solid at the top but hollow at the bottom; high-sounding on the surface but senseless and corrupt underneath." The farce of China's current attempts at proving itself a Republic was evidence of the truth of these assertions. Effective political organizations had to grow out of an integrated social system. Such a social system could initially take root only in "small localities," and in such local settings "it is the individual citizens who comprise the foundation of the citizenry as a whole." To Mao this had to be a voluntaristic process: "A forced attempt at construction simply will not work." Mao then drew on the discussions of Marxism he had attended in Beijing but suggested that some of those arguments were lacking in cogency. People had used the example of Lenin, wrote Mao, to argue that "political organizations can reform social organizations," and that "group forces can transform the individual." Mao felt Lenin's example in Russia was a special case, not one that could be simply applied to China. For a start, Lenin had relied on "millions of party members" to undertake his "unprecedented course of popular revolution that made a clean sweep of the reactionary parties and washed away the upper and middle classes." Lenin had a carefully thought-out ideology—Bolshevism—and a "reliable mass party" that carried out his orders "as smoothly as flowing water." The peasants of Russia also responded to his revolutionary call. Were there to be a "thorough and general revolution in China," Mao wrote, he would support it. But he knew that was not possible at the moment. Accordingly, he would work for a Republic of Hunan "that shines like the rising sun."

Events, however, were pushing China away from the federation of provinces that Mao envisioned. Part of the problem was that Hunan was in no way united, and within a few months of Mao's return to Changsha from Shanghai, rival warlords were once again vying for control; although the province did declare its formal independence in November 1920 and formulated its own Hunanese constitution, including the granting of full civil rights to women, the Hunan assembly never established a fully independent jurisdiction. Equally fateful were developments in the Soviet Union. In March 1919 Lenin convened the first meetings of a "Third Communist International" to replace the Second International, which had disintegrated during World War I. This new international—known as the Comintern—was to be the global arm of the Soviet Communist Party, fostering revolution overseas not only to spread the cause of the world's proletarians, but also to strengthen the Soviet Union's own defenses. In the spring of 1920 the first of the Comintern agents (one of them was a Chinese raised in Siberia, who acted as interpreter) arrived in China to speed the formation of a Chinese Communist Party. The Soviet group rapidly identified the *New Youth* editors Li Dazhao and Chen Duxiu as the two most prominent Chinese intellectuals interested in Marxism. Having conferred with Li in Beijing, they traveled to Shanghai to visit Chen. Though the Soviet agents did not meet Mao in either Beijing or Shanghai, and Mao had already returned to Changsha by August 1920 when a Communist "small group"—the first in China—was established in Shanghai, he and his fellow Hunanese had nevertheless made enough of an impression on the inner circle of leading radicals for Changsha to be included among the six cities in which further Communist "small groups" were to be formed. (The other four cities were Beijing, Wuhan, Jinan in Shandong province, and Canton.)

The first brief "Manifesto" of the Chinese Communist Party appeared in Shanghai in November 1920, but there is no evidence that Mao saw it right away. From a flurry of letters that Mao wrote at this time to friends in many parts of China and in France, we know that he was frantically busy with his teaching, running the New People's Study Society and the Cultural Book Society, building up a "rent-a-book readers' club," and coordinating the struggle for Hunanese independence. Mao does not mention the Manifesto to any of his November correspondents, so it is unlikely that he had seen it yet or had any hand in drafting it. To a woman student friend from Changsha, who was then in France, Mao expressed his pessimism over the Hunanese people's capacity for change, but added philosophically, "Education is my profession, and I have made up my mind to stay in Hunan for two years." Mao was also clearly thinking deeply about his relationship with Yang Kaihui, struggling to avoid the entanglements and hypocrisies of what in an unusually frank letter he called the "capitalist" type of marriage in which fear and "legalized rape" were combined. The loftier goal must always be to develop a meaningful union based on "that most reasonable thing, free love," wrote Mao to another friend on November 26. He added: "I have long since declared that I would not join this rape brigade. If you don't agree with me, please put into writing your opposing views."

The November 1920 Chinese Communist Manifesto — as if echoing its Comintern origins — was a formulaic document couched at the theoretical level, with no roots of any kind in the realities of Chinese society. The ideals of the Party were stated as being the "social and common ownership and use of the means of production," abolition of the state, and formation of a classless society. The goals were to overthrow capitalism through class struggle. The immediate task of the Communist Party was to strengthen the anticapitalist forces and "organize and concentrate" the forces of class struggle: workers, peasants, soldiers, sailors, and students were singled out as the troops to be mobilized, and a "general federation of industrial associations" was seen as a central tool of this process. A final general strike would lead to the overthrow of the capitalists and the formation of the dictatorship of the proletariat, under whose leadership the class struggle would continue against "the residual forces of capitalism."

Though the language was vague, the issues here were major, and we know that even before he saw the Manifesto, Mao was beginning to discuss such revolutionary issues through correspondence with several of his Changsha friends, who were now in France on the work-study program. In two especially long and detailed letters, one of December 1, 1920, and another of January 21, 1921, Mao wrestled with the two differing views on China's future that the Chinese students in France had divided over. One group pushed for the theory of the dictatorship of the proletariat and the need for violent class struggle. Anarchism, they felt, would not work, the forces of reaction were just too strong. A strong Communist Party, they argued, must be the "initiator, propagandist, vanguard, and operational headquarters of the revolutionary movement." The other group wanted "a moderate revolution," on evolutionary principles, driven by education, focusing on the people's welfare, and using trade unions and cooperatives as its means. Mao was torn: "In principle I agree with the ideas to seek the welfare of all by peaceful means, but I do not believe they will work in reality." Mao had listened to Bertrand Russell when the British philosopher came to Changsha on November 1, 1920, and argued for Communism but against "war and bloody revolutions"; Mao had strenuous arguments about the lecture with his friends and concluded, "This is all very well in theory; in reality it can't be done." A Russian-style revolution was certainly a "last resort" for China, but maybe it was coming to that.

The same issues were being constantly discussed at the Changsha meetings of the New People's Study Society, where the members were overwhelmingly involved in education. Of those who attended regularly in December 1920, according to another of Mao's neat and meticulous reports, besides himself there were three teachers at the Zhounan women's school, three working as editors on the *Popular Newspaper* for a group called "Popular Books and Papers," two teaching at primary school, and two working in the Cultural Book Society; all the others were students: six at middle schools, one at the Hunan-Yale medical school, and one in self-study. None were workers, farmers, or tradespeople. Mao's own feeling was that this group as a whole was "somewhat immature," and showed "childishness in thought and behavior"; some of them were "apt to launch or support causes rashly." He did not entirely exempt himself from criticism. He knew full well that he was "weak-willed," he told a friend in January 1921. "I constantly have the wrong attitude and always argue, so that people detest me." But when Mao convened a lengthy meeting of the Cultural Book Society in that same month and called for a vote on the political options, twelve members, including Mao and Tao Yi, voted for Bolshevism, one voted for moderate (Russell-style) Communism, and two for parliamentary democracy. Tao Yi also spoke out for concentrating on ideological work within the army, rather than putting faith in education throughout the society as a whole. (Yang Kaihui is not listed among the attendants at the meetings.)

Even as the first Comintern agents were exploring the possibilities in China, Lenin convened the Second Congress of the Comintern. Despite serious differences over how to interpret the opportunity in China and what organizational forms would be most suitable, this congress decided to send the Dutch Communist Sneevliet (who operated under the pseudonym "Maring") to China—specifically to Shanghai—to investigate the situation there and elsewhere in Asia. This decision was finalized in August 1920, but due to various organizational problems Maring left for China only in April 1921. His instructions were confusing and contradictory. Following current Comintern policies, he should encourage Chinese Communists to *unite* with the bourgeoisie in the interests of the national revolution, while at the same time leaving room for the development of a strong proletarian organization that could eventually *overthrow* the bourgeoisie. For his entire trip to China, Maring was given £4,000 sterling, of which he used £2,000 immediately for his wife's expenses and some other political obligations. He also lost £600 of his funds in a bank failure, and was thus left with funding of exactly £1,400 for the entire revolutionary journey. Taking a train from Berlin in April 1921, he obtained his visa for China in Vienna, and traveled from there to Venice, where a passenger ship was readying to sail for China.

Maring reached Shanghai on June 3 and took rooms with a Russian landlady in the International Settlement. Within a few days he made contact with another Comintern representative, Nikolsky, who had been sent from Irkutsk. Though the details are obscure, it appears that Maring coordinated with Communists from the Shanghai and Beijing small groups, who had already begun to plan a Communist conference, and that letters were sent to Communists in the other four cities where small groups had formed, as well as to a Communist living in Japan and one with no fixed affiliation living in Hong Kong. Thus it was, after various delays and mishaps, that fifteen representatives (thirteen Chinese and the two Comintern representatives) convened in Shanghai for the First Congress of the Chinese Communist Party on July 23, 1921. The fifteen were there to represent the complete roster of fifty-three Chinese Communists who were then affiliated with the Party in some form or other.

Mao was one of the two invited to come from the Changsha small group, a fact that was to prove crucial to his subsequent revolutionary career. But why was he chosen? There is no absolutely clear answer. As we have seen, Mao knew the Party founders, Li Dazhao and Chen Duxiu, at least fairly well, and had made a name for himself in Changsha educational circles. He also knew the Yangs and a fairly wide circle of influential

Hunanese. But he had virtually no formal knowledge of social-ist ideology, and it was not until January 1921 that he even mentioned "the materialist conception of history" in his writ-ings. Mao derived his new interest in Marxism partly from cor-responding with his friends in France, some of whom had joined the Communist Youth League there, and from reading a new magazine, *The Communist*, developed by Li Da and the Communist small group in Shanghai, and published as a monthly underground Party journal for seven issues between November 1920 and July 1921. Mao stated that he admired the journal for its "clear-cut stand," but as far as we can tell from the surviving records he did not sell it in the Cultural Book So-ciety's store. Mao knew little about the proletariat, though he had spoken vaguely of doing some industrial work in a ship-building yard or factory, and at a meeting of the Society in Janu-ary 1921 he had mentioned that he wanted to "learn to do some form of manual labor, such as knitting socks or baking bread." Otherwise he would continue to be a teacher, and perhaps a re-porter as well.

Basically, though, Mao's proven strength was as a business-man. The operations of the Cultural Book Society had grown prodigiously, with sales from a vastly expanded list of titles reaching 4,049 Chinese dollars and expenses of 3,942 dollars for the seven months from September 1920 to the end of March 1921. The business had expanded to encompass seven full county branches of the store, with their own staffs (Mao hoped to have one in each of the seventy-five Hunan counties before too long) and there were also four smaller outlets in local schools, as well as three run by individuals in their own homes. The main office of the company was still in the rented Hunan-Yale building, though the premises had grown too cramped, and Mao was seeking a larger and more central location in Changsha. Mao now called himself by the unusual title of "special negotiator" for the bookstore, and a friend of his from Xiangtan was listed as "manager." Besides these entrepreneurial skills, there was the fact that Mao clearly had remarkable energy and initiative, and a good deal of physical courage. He was handsome too: lean, tall, and with large, mournful eyes. Photos of the time show him with long hair swept dramatically back from his brow. Apparently, Mao was also never at a loss for words. Perhaps the Beijing and Shanghai intellectuals, with their sophisticated knowledge of the world, found something refreshing in this untutored youth from the Hunan backlands.

The July 1921 First Communist Party Congress in Shanghai was tense. The Comintern agent Maring aroused instant dislike among many of the Chinese, and his doctrinaire plans for their future—especially the need to ally with the bourgeoisie—were hotly contested: two of the Chinese present flatly rejected Maring's request that they give him a "work report." Neither Li Dazhao nor Chen Duxiu even attended the Congress, and the proceedings were further disrupted when on July 30 a stranger wandered right into the private house where they were meeting, explaining lamely that he had come to the wrong place. Experienced in holding clandestine meetings and in police procedures, Maring at once suggested the members scatter, which they did, and shortly after that the police arrived. One advantage of this for the Chinese was that they could now state that the presence of two Westerners made their group too conspicuous. Accordingly the last session of the congress was held in a boat on a nearby Zhejiang lake, and Maring and Nikolsky did not attend.

The documents of this first congress were never published,

even for internal distribution within the Party, and no record of the exact nature of Mao's participation has been preserved. A brief summary of the congress was filed in the Comintern archives, though its author and reliability cannot be ascertained. It appears that each of the local groups gave a report on their activities and emphasized the small size of their membership and the need to expand. Maring spoke of his work in Indonesia and underscored the need to develop the labor movement in China; Nikolsky described the founding of the Far Eastern Secretariat of the Comintern in Irkutsk, and also the situation inside the Soviet Union.

The most important discussion seems to have focused on whether to break altogether with bourgeois society or to find a link between open work and secret work that would let the Party operate more openly in society. Congressional delegates argued that workers should be encouraged to "expand their outlook" and take part in "the struggle for freedom of publication and assembly." Open propagation of Communist theories was "an absolute condition for success"—though at the same time it was "futile to hope to build a new society within the old system." Ultimately the working class would have to learn how to liberate itself because it was not possible "to force it to carry out revolution." On the last day of the congress, without the Comintern representatives present, the Chinese argued over what exactly was meant by the proletariat's "allying with other parties and factions," and whether the warlords were the most important enemy. After "short but intense debate" it was recommended that for the immediate future the focus of the Communist Party should be on organizing factory workers. Organizing the peasantry and the army should wait until there were more Party members available—such members should be especially sought out in the working class.

The final "program" of the Party, on which all were said to agree, stated that the capitalist class must be overthrown and a classless society established inside China. Machinery, land, buildings, and other means of production would be under "social ownership." Membership in the Party would not be restricted by gender or nationality. It was enough that each new member have the backing of a preexisting Party member, with background checking of suitability for membership not to exceed two months. Party doctrines and membership lists were to be kept secret. Any area of China where there were five members could form its own unit, called a "Soviet." Soviets with more than thirty members would form their own executive committees. Finances, Party policies, and publications would all be supervised by the Central Committee of the Party, of which Chen Duxiu would be the general secretary.

Mao Zedong was back in Changsha by early August 1921, having been instructed at the congress to build up the Party in Hunan. His first response to this order, in line with his earlier experiences, was to announce on August 16 the formation of a "Hunan Self-Study University." On the surface this was to run somewhat along the lines of the old dynasty's Confucian study academies—it literally met on the premises of one such academy in Changsha that had been founded in the late Qing to propagate the thought of an earlier Chinese patriotic thinker opposed to the Manchu conquest of 1644. This location was made possible by the fact that Mao's fellow Communist delegate from Hunan, the fifty-one-year-old scholar He Shuheng, had been named director of the academy, and the Hunan government had provided it with a monthly stipend of 400 Chinese dollars. The goal of the new university, Mao stated, was to get away from the "mechanical conformity of teaching methods" still all too common, and to form a fully "democratic" community that would "strive to smash the mystery of learning" and be affordable for all. "Correspondents" appointed by the university would keep the students in touch with intellectual developments worldwide (New York, London, Paris, Moscow, and Tokyo were among those places mentioned) and also in schools throughout Hunan. Marxism was not mentioned in the roster of courses, but the university formed a convenient front for recruiting and vetting possible members of the Communist Party, and students enrolling found they were given the choice of taking courses in Marxist-Leninist theory. A similar use was made of a YMCA-sponsored "mass literacy" campaign that happened to be going on in Changsha at the same time, based in public halls, schools, churches, and private homes, which allowed Communist organizers to reach over a thousand potential recruits.

In November, the Party Central Committee specifically mentioned that Changsha must recruit at least twenty new "comrades" to form "district executive committees," and combine with other areas to get at least two thousand young socialist league members. (It was probably around this time that Yang Kaihui joined the Communist Party formally.) The Changsha district was also told to get "more than one labor union under its direct control" and to establish "solid relations" with other labor unions. The short-term goal was for all the districts to unite in forming a national union of railway workers. In line with such specific directives, Mao had already (in September) traveled to the massive Anyuan coal mines just across the border in Jiangxi, pretending to be a tourist, and even went down the colliery shafts. That November, Mao issued a particularly lavish eulogy on the Labor Association of Changsha, which had launched a major strike the previous April, although he had not been involved in its work and it was in fact controlled by Hunanese anarchists.

The Labor Association was bound to become the focus of Mao's attentions, now that his goals had been defined so dramatically. The association already had a following among a wide variety of Hunan operations and laborers—spinning mills, the mint, lead-smelting plants, construction workers, tailors and barbers, machinists and railway workers. In January 1922 it spearheaded a major strike against a Changsha spinning mill, and the military governor of Hunan—the same man who had been Mao's commanding officer after the murder of the secret-society revolutionaries in 1912—responded by sending troops with machine guns to break the strike and also beheaded two student leaders believed to have aided the strikers.

Mao's scale of activities was now broadening swiftly. In the midst of the endless organizational work and the addressing of the somewhat contradictory calls of the Party center, he had managed to spend enough time with Yang Kaihui for them to start a family. Despite the absence of any formal ceremony they now considered themselves married. Their first son, Anying, was born in October 1922. But something curious was happening to Mao. The young man who had struggled so often against the autocratic nature of his father, who hated and despised the shackles of bourgeois marriage and had found joy in a free-love relationship, who detested schools and would never be a student in one again, and who always sought freedom of spirit and the chance to grow and change had willingly accepted, at the age of twenty-eight, a much greater degree of disciplined control from the Communist Party than any he had encountered in his life before.

Workers and Peasants

IN EARLY 1921, Mao was still a political amateur. The meetings of the New People's Study Society, over which he often presided, were attended largely by teachers and their students, who seemed absorbed with such problems as whether or not to found a restaurant to provide cheap food for local workers, and whether their goal should be to "transform China" or to "transform China and the world." By the end of 1922, however, Mao was becoming a professional revolutionary organizer and learning how to coordinate major strikes that affected the lives of tens of thousands of workers.

The first of these was a strike by construction workers and carpenters, who hitherto had been organized along traditional guild lines. At the site of the Hunan Self-Study University in Changsha, Mao got to know some of the carpenters repairing the old buildings. He talked to them about their labor contracts and their pay scales, and persuaded one of the carpenters to join the Communist Party. The choice was a good one, and the chosen carpenter turned out to be a natural leader and a brilliant organizer. Working along with Mao, who had been given the sonorous title by the Party of "Secretary to the Hunan Office of the Secretariat of the Chinese Labor Organization," in September and October 1922 the carpenter led a series of rallies, demonstrations, and work stoppages that brought a major raise in the workers' basic hourly wages.

Another strike, in November 1922, came from the lead-type compositors and printers, who had formed their own union in 1920 but had later split apart along the lines of their specific skills—lithographers, press operators, printers, and typesetters. That Mao was now well known in Changsha for his organizational skills but was not yet perceived to be a dangerous radical can be seen from the fact that in the settlement of the strike that followed, he was called in by the newspaper proprietors as a "mediator." In this role, and with the strong solidarity of the workers behind him, he was instrumental in gaining virtually all of their demands.

In one of the careful synopses of current politics, replete with facts and figures that had become his hallmark, Mao estimated that by early 1923 there were twenty-three major workers' organizations in Hunan, with a membership of around 30,000 workers. In the same period there had been ten strikes, involving a total of 22,250 workers, of which nine were "victorious or semi-victorious." In addition to the two above, Mao included in his list of workers' organizations miners (in coal, zinc, and lead mines), railway employees, machine-shop operators, mint workers, garment workers, silk factory employees, electrical workers, barbers, boot- and shoemakers, and rickshaw pullers. Mao himself had been involved in the strategic planning of several of these other strikes, some of which had been led and directed by his former Changsha schoolmates, now returned from their work-study experience in France (where several of them had already joined the Communist Youth League or the Communist Party). Mao's two younger brothers were also active in strike work, one as the organizer of a consumer cooperative in the collieries, and the other in the workers' club at the lead mines. And Mao's wife, Yang Kaihui—though pregnant with their first child—had been working among the peasants who lived near the areas where the miners had been on strike, helping to push for women's rights and better educational facilities. It was an impressive record.

The world of Hunanese activism, however, was not the center of Communist Party politics as a whole. Under instructions from the Comintern, and with Maring still in China to see that the orders were followed, the Chinese Communist Party was being pushed into an alliance with Sun Yat-sen's Guomindang Nationalist Party. Mao was almost certainly among the Communists who found this a dangerous policy: he was learning that workers were building up their own solidarity against the forces of the bourgeoisie, and even against the foreigners, though the antagonism of the militarists—who could be the most savage of strikebreakers—was unpredictable and had already wreaked havoc in Hunan. Also, as an early member of the Party, it was hardly up to him to protest publicly. Chen Duxiu, however, whom Mao had so long admired, had no such inhibitions. Chen listed a number of reasons for his opposition to Maring's plans that the Communists should join with the Nationalists, such as the completely different aims and policies of the two parties, and the fact that the Nationalist Guomindang was cooperating actively with the United States and northern warlords, as well as corrupt pro-Japanese politicians, so that to join them would drive all the youth away from their "faith" in the Communist Party. Chen added that the Nationalists had no tolerance for the ideas of new members and "used lies as power."

The Second Communist Party Congress, at which these

and other crucial issues concerning the role of the proletariat in the current struggle were discussed, had convened in Shanghai from July 16 to 23, 1922. Presumably Mao was invited to be there, since he had attended the First Congress, and had been serving ever since as head of the Hunan labor secretariat, with success. Yet he missed the meetings altogether. The only explanation that he ever gave, many years later, was a curious and incomplete one: "I forgot the name of the place where it was to be held, could not find any comrades, and missed it." It is certainly true that on some earlier occasions Mao had admitted to being somewhat scatterbrained—he once told a correspondent that he had lost his letter in the middle of reading it—but the explanation remains strange. Mao knew Shanghai fairly well by this time, after three visits of which two were fairly lengthy, and had many Party contacts. On the other hand, one could argue, Shanghai was a huge city subdivided into many subsections, including two international settlements; Yang Kaihui was five months pregnant; he had been overworked for a long time; and several other delegates also missed the meeting, including Li Dazhao and the whole Canton delegation. The twelve delegates attending reached enough consensus about the need for a Communist alliance with the bourgeoisie to issue a statement agreeing that they would cooperate with Sun Yat-sen and other Guomindang Nationalist Party leaders.

There were various reasons for this decision, besides Party loyalty to the dictates from Moscow. A massive strike of seamen in Hong Kong in which the Nationalist organizers had been active had ended triumphantly for the workers in May 1922, raising the Guomindang's prestige as an inherently revolutionary organization. Despite the strike successes the Communist Party itself was still dangerously small: the twelve delegates in

1922 represented a total China-wide Communist membership of 195, a fourfold increase from the year before but hardly an overwhelming number. Besides, of the 195, only around thirty were workers. Also, the Communist Party in China had almost no money whatever. Most of the members had no jobs or other sources of income. Expenses for the central organs of the party during the fall and winter of 1921 to 1922 had totaled 17,500 Chinese dollars, of which the Comintern provided 16,665 dollars. The projected budget for the following year was all expected to come from the same Comintern sources. However, it was only after another special meeting, convened by Maring at Hangzhou in August 1922, that it was made mandatory for all Communists to *join* the Guomindang Nationalist Party, as what was called "a bloc within." Many of the Communist leaders joined right away, including Li Dazhao and even Chen Duxiu, despite the earlier misgivings. Mao, however, seems to have delayed joining the Nationalist Party until early in 1923. Perhaps the final spur for him was the savage suppression in February 1923 of the railway workers' union by a northern warlord in whose progressive potential the Communist Party had once believed. Many workers were killed, and the union leader was publicly beheaded. Clearly the dangers confronting the workers from militarists were nationwide, and Hunan was no different from anywhere else. By the summer of 1923, Mao was definitely a member of the Nationalist Party. Yet despite this new alliance, growth for the Communists continued to be slow and difficult, with the Party membership climbing only up to 420 by June 1923, of whom 37 were women, 164 were workers, and 10 were in jail.

Mao's career trajectory now began to change, as he was caught up in the swirl of official political business. Though

Yang Kaihui was pregnant again by the spring of 1923, Mao had to leave home in June to attend the Third Congress of the Communist Party. This one was held in Canton—Mao did not get lost, though he had not visited the city before—and he dutifully endorsed the declarations concerning alliance with the Guomindang. At this congress Mao was elected to the Communist Party's ruling Central Executive Committee, and named head of the Party's organization department. Though a major advancement, the latter post had its problems for family life, as Mao had to proceed to Shanghai, which he reached in July. The news from Changsha was alarming. A new militarist clamped his hold over the city, new levels of violence erupted in Hunan, many schools were closed, and several of the unions Mao himself had helped to found the year before were suppressed. Dramatically reversing the position on Hunan's independence he had taken not so long before, Mao as a Party spokesman now wrote, "We have always opposed a federation of self-governing provinces," on the grounds that it would simply be "a federation of military governors in their separatist regimes."

In September, Mao left Shanghai to rejoin his wife and reached Changsha on September 16, 1923. There he found two major armies drawn up facing each other along the Xiang River, and was so nervous for his family that he routed his political correspondence via a private courier and asked his political contacts to write to him under an assumed name. Mao also found he could not afford the new tasks that had fallen on his shoulders. He told his contacts in the Nationalist Party that he would need at least 100 Chinese dollars each month to run the operation they envisioned in Changsha, and to rent the necessary office space. It was in these rather dispiriting circumstances that Yang Kaihui and Mao's second child was born, sometime in November 1923—another boy, whom they named Anqing.

Mao stayed with Yang Kaihui through December, skipping the Communist Central Executive Committee's meeting that he should have attended in Shanghai. Instead, he sent the committee a pessimistic report on the Hunan situation. Mao noted in the report that peasant organizations—formerly reaching up to ten thousand members in the area south of Changsha—led by the Socialist Youth League, had been crushed, partly because of an extremist policy of "economic agitation" that alienated even the moderately prosperous middle peasants, and partly because of counterforce from the militarist's troops. Only fourteen people had joined the Communist Party in Changsha during the previous four months, and another thirty or so in strike centers outside the city. Widespread closure of Changsha's factories due to the incessant warfare had impoverished the workers, and the workers' clubs had all closed down or become totally inactive.

But even if Party leaders had excused Mao's absence in December, new orders from the Comintern to forge a United Front with the Guomindang made it imperative for him to attend the first National Guomindang Congress, scheduled for January 1924 in Canton. Mao must have felt he had no choice but to go. Yang Kaihui, though a Communist Party member herself, clearly felt it was Mao's duty to stay with her and the two children, now aged fourteen months and one month, trapped in a war-torn city. Though there are no surviving personal letters between Mao and Yang, Mao had kept his love of Chinese poetry ever since his schooldays, and used poems to express his private emotions to his close friends. It is a poem to Yang Kaihui, dating from December 1923, which, despite its formal meter and cross-references to other poems from the classical canon, gives us the clearest view of their tangled emotions at this intensely difficult moment in their lives:

> Waving farewell, I set off on my journey.
> The desolate glances we give each other make things
> worse,
> Yet again emphasizing our bitter feelings.
> Eyes and brows reflect your tension,
> As you hold back hot tears that seek to flow.
> I know you have misunderstood our past exchanges;
> What drifts before our eyes are clouds and fog,
> Even though we thought none knew each other as well
> as you and I.
> When people feel such pain,
> Does Heaven know?
>
> At dawn today, thick frost on the way to East Gate,
> A fading moon and half the sky reflected in our patch of
> pond—
> Both echo our desolation.
> The sound of the train's whistle cuts straight through
> me.
> From this time on I'll be everywhere alone.
> I'm begging you to sever these tangled ties of emotion.
> I myself would like to be a rootless wanderer,
> And have nothing more to do with lovers' whispers.
> The mountains are about to tumble down.
> Clouds dash across the sky.

January 1924 in Canton was frenetic for Mao. He took an active part in the key political debates, became familiar with the new figures in the political scene, and showed an ability to concentrate a discussion and bring it to a vote in an effective yet consensus-building way. After the congress, Mao was elected an alternate member of the Guomindang's own Central Executive Committee, and he attended four successive meetings of the Guomindang Central Party Bureau, again making substantive suggestions on funding and administrative procedures. From February through the fall of 1924, Mao was stationed in Shanghai, working both in senior Guomindang positions (where he also kept the minutes) and in his Communist Party positions; much of his work centered on making the United Front a reality, by defining the role that members of each party should play in the proceedings of the other, a delicate and demanding job, and one with dangers of misapprehension by both sides. In June 1924, Yang Kaihui came to join him in Shanghai, at least for a time. (They had a nanny now, to help them with the two children.)

By July, Mao was growing convinced that the Guomindang alliance with the Communists might not be tenable much longer, and with Chen Duxiu he cosigned a position paper to the Communists, urging them to consider the contingency of withdrawing. The Guomindang right wing was gaining ground, they argued, and intent on placating the militarists and the merchants by suppressing movements of the workers and peasants. Mao signed a second important circular on September 10, concerning warlords in central China, and a third in November on party work and policies toward Sun Yat-sen. Then suddenly, in December, Mao pulled out altogether and went home to Changsha. In February 1925 he traveled deeper into the countryside, back to his native village of Shaoshan in Xiangtan county. For almost a year he attended no meetings of either political party, and was dropped from his important committees one by one.

Mao told his Communist superiors that he was exhausted,

and there is no need to doubt it. He also, one may assume, wanted to spend time with his family. A third reason—though where to place it in terms of the other two is unclear—was that he wanted to work with the peasants on his own former home turf, where he knew their ways and their dialects, their tragedies and their hopes. A corollary to that reason would be that Mao wanted to build a base of his own, in a region and among people he trusted and understood. Even though, in a rather abstract way, the Comintern and the Communist Party (and even the Guomindang) had espoused the cause of peasant liberation with various degrees of rhetoric, those pronouncements were no substitute for trying to understand rural China on the ground that one knew best. Elsewhere in China, especially on the southeast coast, a few other pioneers had embarked on the formation of peasant associations and cooperatives or had begun to push for some release from harsh tenantry terms, or even for redistribution of land. Yang Kaihui may have shared this interest, and certainly there had been several experiments in Hunan—their extent, as well as their collapse, had been reported by Mao (in absentia) to the Communist Central Executive Committee in late 1923.

During this time, Mao did not write about his experiences in the countryside, and his usual spate of journalistic reportage came to a complete halt. He seemed to have at last abandoned the roles of reporter and teacher that he had declared to be his lifelong ambitions back in 1921 at the New People's Study Society meetings. The silence is complete from December 1924 through October 1925; but that October he returned to Guangzhou suddenly and took up work once again, this time in the Guomindang propaganda department. His pronouncements were once again in favor of the United Front, against imperialism and the militarists, and for the social revolution of the proletariat. In January 1926 he was asked to include his views on the peasantry within the context of a joint report to the Guomindang Congress, but there is still little indication of his recent thinking on the topic, or of his own experiences in Hunan. Then on February 14, 1926, Mao sent a brief note to the Guomindang secretariat stating that his "mental ailment" had "increased in severity," and requesting two weeks' leave. His stand-in was to be Shen Yanbing (later, under the name Mao Dun, to be one of China's most celebrated Communist writers).

Shen later noted that Mao took this brief leave to go back to Hunan to check on the potential of the peasant movement there. If that was accurate, it shows Mao's "mental ailment" was a specious excuse, and his political focus beginning to coalesce. From this time forward, Mao's rural activism manifested itself in numerous ways, starting with propaganda work for the Communists and the Guomindang, continuing with his summaries of the role of the Chinese peasants in various revolutionary settings of the past, and on to his own return to teaching, this time as the director of the classes in the Peasant Training Institute between May and September 1926, in which role his passions for exposition and research could be combined. Mao's field notes from one of his research trips back to his birthplace of Xiangtan county in 1926 show his amazing grasp of detail: in assessing a peasant family budget he calculated not only land acreage and usury rates but also the price and use of lard, salt, lamp oil, tea, seed, and fertilizer, as well as costs and maintenance of draft animals and farm tools. (He subdivided hoes into three categories according to their weight and cost.) Firewood and fuel, clothing and home weaving, winnowing fans and rice sifters—nothing was unimportant to Mao.

This period of Mao's deepening interest in recording—and ultimately changing—the realities of rural China overlapped with momentous changes in Chinese politics. The United Front of the Communists and the Guomindang seemed to be working, and to hold firm even after Sun Yat-sen's death from cancer in 1925. Massive popular movements against foreign imperialism in China came into being in mid-1925, sparked in part by the shooting of civilian Chinese demonstrators by British forces seeking to protect foreign lives and property. Workers began to take a prominent part in politics, and Communist Party membership expanded dramatically: still under a thousand in early 1925, the Communist Party had expanded to over 57,000 members by the spring of 1927.

Aided by Comintern advisers, and by the well-trained junior officers graduating from the military academy that the two parties had established at Whampoa near Canton, both the Communists and the Guomindang rapidly expanded their military base as well. Chiang Kai-shek, a former trusted aide to Sun Yat-sen, and the commandant of the Whampoa military academy, swiftly emerged as a dominant force in the Guomindang armies and built up his own fanatically loyal following among the recently graduated young officers. Despite some inevitable ideological tensions, the combined Guomindang and Communist armies moved out of Canton under Chiang Kai-shek's overall command in the spring of 1926, in a concerted drive to break the power of the various militarist regimes in China and to reunify the country.

Mao was one of those called on by the United Front to organize peasant forces in the countryside to help this northern expedition on its way, and by August 1926 the United Front armies had swept into Changsha. That fall they routed the remaining Hunan militarists and reached the Yangtze River. Mao partook of these sweet tastes of victory. Surely few occasions in his political life could have rivaled the moment on December 20, 1926, when he stood on the stage in the Magic Lantern Theater in Changsha before a cheering audience of over three hundred, as a bell rang at two P.M. to announce the beginning of a speech by "Mr. Mao Zedong, born in Xiangtan, Hunan province. Mr. Mao is a leader of the Chinese revolution, and he has paid particular attention to the peasant movement." Such an experience, Mao told the audience, as he launched into his analysis of the class components of revolution, would have been inconceivable a year before.

On January 4, 1927, Mao began a month-long trip through the Hunan countryside he knew best, including the two counties of Xiangtan and Xiangxiang, birthplaces respectively of his father and his mother. In a forty-page report of sustained passion and excitement which he submitted to the Communist Party in mid-February, Mao described the seizures of power in the area by the poorest of the peasants and the humiliations of the landlords as they were forced to walk, wearing tall conical paper hats of mockery, through the villages they once had dominated. He spoke of the women who seized the chance for independence from their husbands, of the secret-society members and even the petty criminals who found their strength through this new form of rebellion, of the joys of violence and the joys of righting ancient wrongs, and of the children's games now politicized in allegorical form.

It is perhaps the most passionate piece of writing Mao ever did, but even here, as if he could not resist it, he included careful tables with neat rows of figures on the size and location of each peasant association. Xiangxiang county he judged to be the most radical, with 190,544 peasant association members in 499 village groupings; Xiangtan county was fourth, with 120,460 members in 450 village groupings. The only close rival in rhetorical excitement to this report had been Mao's "Great Union of the Popular Masses," written in the summer of 1919. There Mao had written: "From Lake Dongting to the Min River, the tide rides ever higher. Heaven and earth are aroused by it, the wicked are put to flight by it. Ha! We know it! We are awakened! The world is ours, the state is ours, society is ours. If we do not speak, who will speak? If we do not act, who will act? We must act energetically to carry out the great union of the popular masses, which will not brook a moment's delay!" Now in 1927 it was the peasantry of his former home who held China's destiny: "All revolutionary parties and all revolutionary comrades will stand before them to be tested, to be accepted or rejected as they decide. To march at their head and lead them? To stand behind them, gesticulating and criticizing them? Or to stand opposite them and oppose them? Every Chinese is free to choose among the three, but by force of circumstances you are fated to make the choice quickly."

The Long Retreat

IN THE SPRING OF 1927 it all came crashing down. The labor unions in Shanghai were gutted first, in April, by Chiang Kai-shek and his allies among the warlords, who had all grown alarmed over the mounting power of the Communist Party. Working with local secret-society and criminal organizations, and with the open connivance of the Westerners in the international concessions, Chiang ordered a roundup of Communists and labor leaders. Thousands were killed and the Communist movement in the city was almost wiped out. Communist theorists in the Comintern, and Stalin himself, claimed that the terror was a positive development, since it "proved" that the right wing of the Guomindang had shown its counterrevolutionary nature; they insisted, however, that the Chinese Communists continued to work with the "left" wing of the Guomindang, which was based in the industrial tri-city area of Wuhan, inland up the Yangtze. After leaving Changsha, Mao was sent to Wuhan so he could continue working in his capacity as an alternate member of the Guomindang Central Committee; and in an attempt to placate the left Guomindang, the Communist Central Committee ordered Mao to dampen the enthusiasm of the peasant masses he had just been writing so enthusiastically about. By midsummer of 1927, the Wuhan Guomindang leaders had decided to throw in their lot with Chiang Kai-shek and abandon the Communists. At this stage, a new wave of terror and repression of the Communists took place in the Wuhan region, and against the peasant associations there and in Hunan. It was in this grim situation that the Communist Party Central Committee—again reacting to orders from Stalin and the Comintern—ordered Mao to re-fan the flames of peasant insurrection, so as to move the revolution to a higher stage.

Not surprisingly, Mao found the task impossible. In his excited Hunan report of February 1927 he had tallied up a total of 1,367,727 members of the peasant associations in the province of Hunan alone. Now, in August 1927, away from the base area he knew best, and in the midst of massive military repression, Mao could raise only a few thousand followers. Most of them were killed or routed by local militarists after brief campaigns.

One thing that Mao did learn at this time was the importance of having adequate military force to back up one's political goals. There had been hints of his thinking on this matter before, but it was in a report on August 7, 1927, that he first gave it concrete expression. Mao opened by commenting on the now defunct Guomindang alliance, in terms that unmistakably echoed his feelings about the young Changsha bride whose suicide in 1919 had prompted some of his finest early writing. All of the Communists had been mistaken, he wrote, in thinking "that the Guomindang belonged to others. We did not realize that it was an empty house waiting for people to move in. Later, like a maiden getting into the bridal sedan chair, we reluctantly moved into this empty house, but we never made up our mind to play the host there." Only when it was too late did the Communist leadership try to get the peasants and workers to join the Nationalists. His Hunan report "had its impact in Hunan," Mao continued, "but it had no influence whatever on the center. The broad masses inside and outside the Party want revolution, yet the Party's guidance is not revolutionary; there really is a hint of something counter-revolutionary about it." Chiang Kai-shek had the right idea—he "rose by grasping the gun." Now it was time for the Communist Party to do the same: "From now on, we should pay the greatest attention to military affairs. We must know that political power is obtained from the barrel of the gun."

By mid-September, Mao and what peasant forces he had been able to muster were narrowly surviving in eastern Hunan. He was still hoping to launch an attack on Changsha, as a prelude to wider uprisings throughout Hunan province, though true to his new insight he was also hoping that two regiments of Communist troops might be dispatched to help him. His tone remained optimistic, but the details of his report did not suggest much hope for the success of a major rising against the strong local militarists who now dominated the region. "Preparations" had been made to cut electric power lines and interdict railroad travel in the area, said Mao, but he gave no specifics of what they were. "The peasants of the suburbs" outside Changsha would constitute the "main force," and they would be supported in turn by the rickshaw pullers in the city, and by "about five hundred wounded soldiers" who were billeted in the city. It was a hopeless scheme and it went nowhere.

In early October, Mao, completely trapped on the border between Hunan and Jiangxi provinces, with nowhere else to go, began discussions with two veteran secret-society leaders who had created their own protected base area about a hundred miles south in the border mountain ranges of Jinggangshan. By late October 1927, the three men had worked out an agreement, and Mao marched south with his remaining peasant forces to join them in their mountain lair. The retreat meant that Mao lost contact with Yang Kaihui and their children. They had just had their third child, another boy, whom they named Anlong. Through one of his younger brothers, however, Mao was able to stay in touch with other Communist leaders in southern Jiangxi, some of whom later brought their own surviving forces to join him at Jinggangshan.

The following year of 1928 marked yet another turning point in Mao's life. He was now cut off from virtually all the sources of authority and all normal career tracks that he had experienced before. He had lost his Party titles from both the Communists and the Guomindang, and a member of the Hunan Communist Party provincial committee who made his way into the Jinggang mountains in March even told Mao — wrongly, it turned out — that Mao had been deprived of his Party membership. He was with peasants, but few of those he was with can have come from his home region of Xiangxiang or Xiangtan, and the harsh mountain terrain was indescribably different from the lusher valley rice-growing regions in which he grew up. His secret-society allies may have had some Communist sympathies, but the rules with which they ran their mountain world were their own. When Mao was forced, on Party orders, to lead some of his troops down into the plains, they suffered serious reverses and he soon pulled back to his mountain base. On at least one occasion he flatly rejected an order that he make another such military sortie. In a brief report of May 1928 to the Jiangxi provincial committee, Mao gave his "permanent mailing address" as being care of the secret-society leaders in the border mountain region — there was no other way to reach him.

In that same report, Mao mentioned that he and his forces were using the Jiangxi county town of Yongxin as their new "center," and as a base for organizing "insurrections" in the neighboring counties. They needed such a base to bring some order to their motley forces—Mao described his followers as being "a mass of ten thousand messy people with very poor discipline"—and also to develop Party organization, raise money, and make clothes. Yongxin had been a rural revolutionary center since April 1927, when a Communist government was established there. Among well-known local radicals elected to the revolutionary county committee were three younger members of the prominent scholarly and landlord He family, two sisters and a brother, who had all joined the Communist Party the year before, when the Northern Expedition forces were seeking to reunify China. Later the He family joined up with the bandits in Jinggangshan. One of the sisters, He Zizhen, now nineteen, and as famous for her looks as for her spirit, met Mao in the mountains. Mao was thirty-four, lean from privation, rich with experience from his organizational work among the peasantry, and a storehouse of knowledge about Communist and Guomindang Party leaders. He was now living to the fullest—if not entirely by his own choice—that heroic wandering knight-errant life of which he had written to Yang Kaihui in his poem of 1923. Apparently his memories of his wife and small children were fading; in any case, he was trapped in the mountains by opposing armies and had no way of getting to Changsha, nor had Yang Kaihui any way of leaving home and coming to the mountains to join him. A poem Yang Kaihui wrote to Mao in October 1928 reflected her sorrow and frustration at their separation, and at the impossibility of getting messages through to him. She hoped that he had adequate winter clothes, and worried over a foot injury he had sustained before going up into the mountains. She worried, too, over his sleeping far away, uncherished and alone. But by the time she wrote her poem, He Zizhen and Mao were lovers, and their first child was born in 1929.

Contradictory instructions from the Party center and from the Hunan provincial network continued to reach Mao, and the poverty of the Jinggangshan region, its instability, and the shifting numbers of not always reliable troops, made consistent policy difficult. But in the mountains Mao followed an extremely radical policy, one fully attuned both to the insights he had gathered in examining peasant violence in Hunan and to those aspects of Comintern policy that emphasized peasant extremism (as they often but not invariably did). The "land law" of Jinggangshan, as promulgated by Mao in December 1928, stipulated that *all* land should be confiscated from the wealthy, with most of it being distributed directly to the individual peasants, some tilled in common, and some kept for "model farms." After the land redistribution, except for the old, the very young, and the sick, "the rest of the population must be compelled to work." (So had Lord Shang ordered for the subjects of Qin, twenty-five hundred years before, as Mao had written in his first surviving schoolboy essay.) Hillsides with edible-oil plants were to be divided among the peasants, but the revolutionary government would control all bamboo forests. A flat land tax of 15 percent would be levied in most cases. Members of the Red Army would get the same land distributions as other peasants, but in their case the revolutionary government would hire laborers to work the land for the soldiers on duty. Problems among the troops, however, were omnipresent and almost overwhelming. There was no cold-weather clothing, no drugs or medicines to treat the wounded, almost no money for food, and very little arms or ammunition. It was only through the spirit of

"democracy"—sharing the hardships equally, across all levels—
that the situation could be maintained. Guerrilla action against
the enemy was the most successful—to attack only when in superior strength and to avoid needless "dispersion" of the troops
at all costs.

The Jinggangshan period of Mao's life ended in January
1929, when he decided to find a new base area with greater resources and less constant pressure from militarist or Guomindang counterattacks. Mao's final decision was to move to a new
base area in the border zone between eastern Jiangxi and western Fujian provinces. Down from the mountains, Mao found
himself once again subject to pressures from the Party leadership and assaulted for the survival policies he had followed.
One particularly sharp injunction told Mao to "leave the army"
and report to Shanghai for instructions. Mao prevaricated, and
in an unambiguous response to the Party center told them it
would be a serious mistake "to fear the development of the
power of the peasants lest it outstrip the workers' leadership
and become detrimental to the revolution." A series of crucial
Party meetings were held in western Fujian (Mao had still not
gone to Shanghai, as instructed), and Mao's positions on the
rural revolution and the role of military force came under
fierce criticism.

Mao was ill at this time, once again; this does not seem to
have been a "diplomatic" illness, as on occasions in his past,
but a debilitating combination of poor food, exhaustion, and
malaria. It was also at this time, in Fujian, that their first child,
a baby girl, was born to Mao and He Zizhen. Mao's illness continued through November, and it was in that month that he
wrote a brief letter to his schoolmate and friend Li Lisan, now a
powerful member of the Politburo and soon to be head of the

Party. "I have been ill for three months," wrote Mao, "and although I am better now, my spirits are not yet fully recovered." One explanation for this flatness, Mao went on, was that despite the company of He Zizhen he missed his first wife and children: "I often think of Kaihui, Anying, and the others, and would like to communicate with them, but I don't know their mailing address." Mao asked Li Lisan to seek out Mao Zemin, his younger brother, in Shanghai, and to get Yang Kaihui's address, so that Mao could write to her.

There is no surviving letter from Mao to Yang Kaihui, so we do not know if he ever wrote. What we do know is that shifts in Communist policy, under what came to be called the "Li Lisan Line" of renewed assaults on cities, led in October 1930 to a Communist assault on Changsha, where Yang Kaihui was living privately with the three small children and their nanny. The Communist attack was a failure, and in the mopping-up operations conducted by the Guomindang militarists that followed, one of the Guomindang generals heard of Yang Kaihui's presence in the city and of her relationship with Mao. He arrested and interrogated her, and when she refused to renounce Mao, had her shot. The three children and their nanny were bailed out by friends and sent back to Shanghai, where the children were enrolled in a kindergarten. After the school closed down, they lived hand-to-mouth for years. The youngest one died, but in 1936 the Communist Party located Anying and Anqing, by then in their early teens, and they were sent to the Soviet Union for safety. Mao was reunited with them only in 1946.

The new base area that the Communists finally established, on the Fujian border with Jiangxi, was known as the Jiangxi Soviet, and it was here that Mao spent most of the next five years. The Jiangxi base area, though far larger than Jinggangshan, was also more vulnerable to attack. For virtually the entire period between 1930 and 1934 it was subjected to repeated assaults by Chiang Kai-shek, who was determined to obliterate this main symbol of Communist survival. As had been the case during the period between 1924 and 1927, Mao was again part of a larger political world, with its own rhythms and imperatives, one that sometimes followed the logic of local circumstances and at other times responded to the dictates of the Comintern. Mao was in partial political eclipse much of this time, though another of his meticulous local examinations—his third after Hunan and Jinggangshan—was devoted to exploring the precise nature of rural life in the Jiangxi county of Xunwu, and constitutes one of the major documents of Communist social analysis for this period. In this report Mao assembled information not only on land relations and class structures in Xunwu, but also telegraph and postal services, the flow of business products (both local and foreign), butchers and wine sellers, herbal medicines and tobacco use, lodging houses and barbershops, the wearing of jewelry, the numbers of prostitutes and their clients, literacy rates, and the handling of adultery.

Mao's career and Party standing fluctuated violently during these years. Much of the time, as titular "chairman" of the provisional Soviet area government, he was the signatory of major Party documents and the convener of meetings, which now had to deal not only with land, labor, and the problem of the militarists, but also with the emerging menace of Japan, which had attacked Shanghai in early 1932 and had taken over the whole of Manchuria. Anti-Japanese nationalism was a potent factor in the Communist Party's recruitment drives, particularly among the patriotic students. But especially after the senior Communist leadership were forced to abandon Shanghai because of the unrelenting Guomindang police pressure there, and moved to the Jiangxi Soviet, Mao found himself on the sidelines, or else had his recommendations completely overruled. On one occasion he was removed from a committee chairmanship in the middle of a meeting.

On several occasions during this period, Mao took "sick leave," as he had in the past. Undoubtedly, some of these absences were political ones, and others were more in the nature of compassionate leave—as when He Zizhen had their second child in 1932, which was delivered in a Fujian hospital by a Communist doctor who had once worked with Mao in Jinggangshan. This child, a boy, they named Anhong. Mao and He Zizhen had left their first child, a daughter, with a rural couple in Fujian, so that she would be safe from the fighting, but she died as an infant. Their third child, born in 1933, seems also to have died in infancy. Mao had health problems, too. The malaria that had troubled him before returned for a while, and in late 1932 he was diagnosed as having tuberculosis, and spent several months in a Fujian sanatorium in the Soviet area before the disease was checked. On various occasions, too, he retreated to isolated scenic sites in the hills with He Zizhen; "bodyguards" were assigned to accompany them, though whether the guards were meant to protect them in case of enemy attack, or constituted a thinly veiled type of house arrest ordered by Mao's rivals within the Communist Party, is not clear. From April to October 1934, though Mao was technically still chairman of the border region government, he and He Zizhen lived together with their baby son in a hillside temple in what was described as "almost complete isolation."

During this period, the attacks from Chiang Kai-shek's forces became so relentless that the Communist Party leadership decided, secretly, that they would have to abandon their base.

Mao was not involved in the planning of this all-important event in Chinese Communist history, the first step in what was later to be called "the Long March." He and his wife joined the great column of some 86,000 fleeing Communist troops and supporters only as it passed near their residence on October 18. About 15,000 Communist troops had been ordered to stay behind in the Soviet, to protect the approximately 10,000 sick or wounded soldiers who could not make the march and to guard the civilian population as well as they could. Mao insisted to Party leaders that He Zizhen—who was once again pregnant—be allowed to make the march with him. There was only a handful of other women on the march, mainly the wives or companions of senior Party leaders, but the couple were not allowed to take their two-year-old son, Anhong, with them. So they entrusted him to Mao's younger brother Mao Zetan, who was among those staying with the rearguard group. When Zetan in turn had to go away on combat duty, he left the two-year-old with one of his bodyguards. Mao Zetan was subsequently killed in the fighting—in 1935—and the boy was never heard of again.

The Long March, later presented as a great achievement in Communist history, was a nightmare of death and pain while it was in progress. The huge column was bogged down with equipment, party files, weaponry, communications equipment, and whatever else had been salvaged from Jiangxi to help them in setting up a new base area. A devastating attack by the Guomindang artillery and air force as the slow-moving column was trying to cross the Xiang River in northern Guangxi province, took close to half their number in casualties. But the march continued, even though there was no agreement on exactly where they were heading, or even on which direction they should take. The leaders, however, had reached a tacit under-standing that when they reached Zunyi, a prosperous city in Guizhou province, they would pause and take stock.

The "Enlarged Meeting of the Politburo" as it was termed, assembled in Zunyi on January 15, 1935, in a crisis atmo-sphere. Party policy had clearly been disastrous, and the very survival of the revolutionary movement hung in the balance. It was a time both to apportion blame for what had gone wrong and—more important—decide what to do in the immediate fu-ture, and who was to lead the Party in doing it. Present at the meetings were seventeen veteran leaders of the Party, including Mao, one Comintern representative, Otto Braun, one inter-preter (for Braun), and a notetaker—the thirty-year-old Deng Xiaoping. In terms of assigning blame, the meeting faulted Braun and two of the Chinese Communist leaders for adopting an overly static defense in the Jiangxi Soviet, one relying often on positional warfare and the construction of blockhouses, rather than on swift deployment and mobile warfare, in which superior Communist strength could have been focused on points of Guomindang weakness. Lack of imagination by the same leaders, the majority concluded, made them miss their chance of linking up with a rebellion of Chiang Kai-shek's troops that broke out in Fujian during 1933. As to immediate goals, the Party should drop the idea of having a base in Guizhou, and instead should cross the Yangtze River and set up a new base in Sichuan province. In terms of Party leadership, there had indeed been "erroneous leadership," but there was "not a split in the Party." The "Group of Three" who had been coordinating the Long March up to this point was abolished, and Mao was named to the Standing Committee of the Polit-buro and given the additional title of "military assistant." Otto

Braun, the Chinese minutes noted, "totally and firmly rejected the criticism of himself."

The Zunyi meetings gave a major boost to Mao's prestige, and it is to this time period that one can date his move toward a commanding position within the Party leadership. But many major problems still had not been resolved. It turned out to be impossible to create the Sichuan base, since Guomindang troops and local militarists kept the Communists from crossing the Yangtze, and after circling aimlessly around Guizhou province for several months, often under fierce enemy attack, they had to swing far down into the south before turning north again along the Tibetan border and heading for their final destination, the sparsely populated northwestern province of Shaanxi. Also, there were still many other major Communist military leaders who were opposed to Mao and saw no reason to risk their own troops for his protection. Some of these commanders not only abandoned Mao and established new base areas of their own, but even lured away some of Mao's finest commanders, so that Mao's forces steadily shrank despite his formal rise in Party status. Finally, in personal terms, there were tragedies. He Zizhen was almost killed in a bombing raid and was left badly injured, with shrapnel embedded in her body in more than a dozen places. Though she subsequently gave birth, to a girl, because of the dangers and pressures of the campaign the baby had to be left with a local peasant family. The girl was thereafter never found, and was the fourth of the children He Zizhen had with Mao Zedong that was lost to them.

During the fall of 1935, Mao's greatly diminished forces endured a hellish march through the swamplands and mountains of Qinghai and Gansu, where their main enemies, apart from grim skirmishes with the local tribespeople, were intense hunger—there was almost no food to be either bought or foraged—the constant damp, and freezing temperatures at night. Many of the remaining 15,000 or so people in the column died of malnutrition, suppurating sores, or by eating poisonous weeds and berries. Only between 7,000 and 8,000 of the column survived, reaching the village of Wayabao in Shaanxi, just south of the Great Wall, in October 1935, and joining forces with some other Communist troops who had already made a base there.

It had been an exhausting and astonishing year since they left Jiangxi, and now Mao had to chart out in his mind a new course for the Communists and for his own career. He was also to be a father again. He Zizhen became pregnant for the fifth time after the March ended, and their daughter Li Min was born in the Shaanxi village of Baoan in the late summer of 1936. "The Maos were proud parents of a new baby girl," as Edgar Snow, the first Westerner ever to interview Mao, jotted in his notes at that time. As had not been the case with any of He Zizhen's other children, she and Mao—though separated—were to see Li Min grow up to maturity, marry, and raise two children of her own. Fate granted them at least that measure of continuity.

Crafting the Image

AFTER SOME HUNTING AROUND in Shaanxi for the most practical and defensible location, by the fall of 1936 the Communists had decided to make their headquarters in Yan'an, a fair-sized market town, with good shelter nearby in the cave dwellings that peasants for centuries had built into the soft loess hillsides. Such dwellings were cheap to build and gave good protection from the extremes of heat and cold that afflicted this arid region. And in a countryside almost barren of trees, the need for timber was reduced to some simple framing for a rough screen and door that would shelter the cave dwellers from wind, dust, and the gaze of the outside world.

The fact that Mao lived in such a cave struck visitors to Yan'an as symbolic of his revolutionary simplicity and fervor. In fact, it was an adjustment to circumstances, of a kind he had made many times before in his life, and Mao settled at once into this strangely desolate new home. He had after all lived for most of his life with none of the amenities of the modernizing urban world, though he had tasted them in Shanghai and Canton. He had time, too, to enjoy the company of his new daughter and to relish the news that Communists in Shanghai had been able to track down two of the children he had had with Yang Kaihui long before—Anying, who was now fourteen, and

Anqing, who was thirteen. However, their youngest brother had died some time in those bleak years, and Anqing's health had been badly damaged by his privations. The boys would be sent to Yan'an as soon as it could be safely arranged.

Mao's main preoccupation, inevitably, was preserving what was left of the Communist organization and deepening his own hold on Party power. The rhetoric of hostility to Japan was easy to construct, and sincere. Japan had brought untold problems to China since the war of 1894–95, and in the 1930s had been strengthening its grip over the whole of Manchuria by means of the puppet state "Manchukuo," nominally controlled by the abdicated last emperor of the Qing dynasty, Henry Puyi, but in reality run by the Japanese army and the huge bureaucracy of the Japanese South Manchurian Railway and related businesses. But implementing an effective anti-Japanese policy was a far more difficult problem. Chiang Kai-shek, in a similar situation, had opted for wiping out the Communists before focusing his armies on defeat of the Japanese. The Communists accordingly developed the counterstrategy of urging the whole of China to unite in opposition to the Japanese, and to end the fratricidal civil war of Chinese against Chinese.

A heaven-sent opportunity for the Communists occurred in December 1936. Chiang Kai-shek flew in to Xian—the capital of Shaanxi province—in an attempt to coordinate a final all-out campaign of annihilation against Mao and the Communist survivors. To accomplish this, Chiang needed the total support of the former warlord of Manchuria, Zhang Xueliang, who had been forced out of his homeland by the Japanese occupation in the northeast but still controlled a large and effective military force. In a startling move, instead of agreeing to fight alongside the Nationalists, General Zhang orchestrated a secret coup whereby Chiang Kai-shek was kidnapped in the middle of the night of December 12 and held under arrest, pending the inauguration of some fully articulated program of unified Chinese resistance against Japan. The Communists had been wooing Zhang Xueliang for some time, trying to win him over to their cause, but there is no evidence that they were privy to all the details of the coup. Nevertheless the seizure of Chiang Kai-shek gave them a chance to size up their options: to have Chiang killed, on the grounds that he had long been their implacable enemy; to use him as a bargaining chip to buy time for themselves to push their social programs; to pressure him to withdraw all his troops from Shaanxi; to release him after obtaining agreement on a United Front against Japan.

Mao, who had just been elected to the crucial position of chairman of the Communist Military Council, in addition to his position on the Politburo, had a central role to play in this debate. After tense discussions within the Party Center, with General Zhang, and with Moscow, the Party decided on a modified form of the last option: to strengthen the United Front. Their statement, released on December 19, managed to combine a tone that was both formally polite and yet slightly mocking. Some of this tone recalls the earlier Mao of the pre–Jiangxi Soviet days, as it addressed the Guomindang leaders and their various warlord allies as "respected gentlemen," and pointed out that in anti-Japanese actions, "the pace of the gentlemen from Nanjing has been rather slow." But the brief heart of the document was all business: establish a cease-fire line between the Communists and the Nationalists; immediately convene a peace conference of "all parties, groups, social strata, and armies"—including the Communists—to meet in Nanjing; let a wide range of views be heard on "the issue of making arrangements for Mr. Chiang Kai-shek," as long as the basic priorities of national unification and resistance to Japan were adhered to; and move fast, "so as to prevent the Japanese bandits from sneaking in at this time of national confusion!"

Chiang Kai-shek refused to make the formal public statement supporting a United Front and end to the civil war that the Communists had hoped for, but he did imply that he would change his current policies, and his release on Christmas Day, 1936, was heralded by the Chinese as evidence that the deadlock was over and that some kind of new anti-Japanese alliance would emerge. In January 1937, Mao and the Party Center debated the correct propaganda line that they should take, and decided to hammer away publicly at a few major issues: the Communist Party itself would deny all prior knowledge of the kidnapping and treat it as entirely "an internal matter of the Guomindang Nanjing government." The Communist Party had always wanted a peaceful solution to the impasse and hence did not issue any formal endorsement of General Zhang Xueliang. It nevertheless hoped Zhang would be appointed to lead his own troops along with those of other western warlords—who of course threatened the frail Communist base area—into a major confrontation with Japan. If Chiang refused to do this, and civil war resumed, he would be "solely responsible." This remained the basic Communist approach until Japanese provocations during the "Marco Polo Bridge incident" near Beijing, on July 7, 1937, induced Chiang Kai-shek at last to order a unified national resistance to Japan, in which the Communists would also join. In expressing total "enthusiasm" for this war, the Communists reminded the Chinese people—in language that might have drawn both sighs and sardonic smiles—that "our party has long since shown in word and deed an open, selfless attitude and a readiness to compromise for the common good, which has won the commendation of all."

Mao in Yan'an could hail the war with "enthusiasm," partly because his base area was well insulated from the most desperate areas of the fighting. That took place between the Japanese army and the regular military forces of the Nationalists' Guomindang armies on the north China plain, in Shanghai, and along the Yangtze River. Especially in protracted fighting around Shanghai, the Nationalists suffered immense losses. After the terrible "rape of Nanjing" by the Japanese on December 7, 1937, brought a literal and symbolic end to any myths of Guomindang power in their own capital city, what was left of the main Nationalist forces retreated up the Yangtze River, first to Wuhan and then, when that fell in the summer of 1938, even deeper inland to Chongqing. Thereafter a good deal of the fighting in central China was waged by scattered units of those Communists who had been left behind at the time of the Long March, or the remnants of various other Soviet governments that had coexisted with the Jiangxi Soviet. In the major cities (including Shanghai) the Communist Party fought a clandestine underground war against the Japanese, often at the same time as Nationalist secret agents and their secret-society allies.

In northern China, after the Nationalist retreat, the main brunt of anti-Japanese action was borne by a sprawling Soviet region to the east of Mao's Yan'an base, which covered parts of the provinces of Shanxi, Chahar, and Hebei. This base was within the reach of aggressive Japanese commanders, and fighting there was vicious, with no quarter given by either side. In both north China and central China (as previously in Manchukuo) the Japanese set up puppet regimes under nominal

Chinese control, with collaborationist troops and police to control the local population, hunt down Communists, and collect taxes. Hundreds of millions of Chinese had little choice but to live under one of the collaborationist regimes; of those who chose to leave their homes and jobs, a majority trekked south and west to join the Nationalists in Chongqing or in the new "United University" that had been formed in Yunnan province by the students and faculty of various prestigious Beijing and Shanghai colleges. Tens of thousands, however, made the equally arduous trek to the north, seeing Yan'an as a place where their talents would be most needed, and Mao as a leader who could focus China's resistance to Japan more effectively than Chiang Kai-shek.

Mao's completion of the Long March, and the factional battles he had fought there, had brought him a leadership position in the Party, but it was by no means unchallenged. His rivals within the Party were numerous and determined, and were constantly refighting the ideological battles of the past in an attempt to apportion blame for prior catastrophes. Mao himself had done this on the Long March, in Zunyi, but in Yan'an the arguments became sharper and more formal. One of Mao's rivals pointed out that though there had been successes in the development of the Red Army, and in the confiscation and redistribution of land, the negative side of the equation was far stronger: "In the white areas, in the cities, and among the workers, we have suffered great losses. Not only did we fail to build up our own forces or prepare for the uprising, but we were tremendously weakened organizationally. Hundreds of thousands of Party members lost their lives. Moreover, tens of thousands of our people are still imprisoned by the Guomindang." Because of "the immaturity and low theoretical level of the Party," the critic continued, the factional struggles within the Party were deeply damaging. Party behavior was "exactly like someone who, never having drunk before, downs a bottle of brandy the first time he touches liquor. . . . The popular term is overkill." Such arguments were historical and technical, but they focused on many of the kinds of policies that Mao had followed in his more extreme moments. Only a few months later, in November, a large group of Russian-trained Chinese Communists returned to Yan'an, and Mao once again found himself involved in swirling levels of technical debate and analysis.

To hold his own in such dangerous eddies, Mao had to sharpen his grasp of Communist dialectic. Though he had of necessity read some Marxist-Leninist literature, he had never received any formal training, either in Party schools or overseas. With his decision, first made in December 1935, to openly challenge the returnees from the Soviet Union, Mao would have to undertake systematic study. Visitors to his cave noted that he was using this post–Long March respite to read books on economics and philosophy. Mao also took other steps to increase his self-image within the Party. On June 22, 1937, for the first time in Mao's life, a portrait of him was published; it appeared in the revolutionary Yan'an newspaper *Liberation*. Mao was shown full face, with a background of troops marching under waving banners. Mao's face, in the picture, was illuminated by the rays of the sun, while under the portrait was printed one of his "sayings," calling for liberation of the Chinese nation and society. In the fall of 1937, young supporters of Mao began to compile a collection of Mao's short works for publication, with an adulatory essay. No Chinese Communist leader's works had ever been published in this way.

Also during that spring and summer of 1937, Mao gave a

short series of lectures on dialectical materialism to students in the revolutionary university, though he admitted that he himself had only just begun to study the problem (and later scholars have shown the lectures were plagiarized from Chinese translations of some Soviet essays on Marxism). What is original about the lectures, however, is that they show Mao beginning to grope for a way to adjust Marxist philosophy to certain realities in the Chinese situation, just as Lenin had adjusted it to certain Russian realities. But this idea was presented only in a fragmentary and incomplete way.

If Mao was to become the accepted leader of his Party, he not only had to win on the battlefield and have successful policies for rural and urban revolution, he also had to be able to hold his own as a theorist. It was as a theorist that he most needed help, and this is where he got it. In the summer of 1937, slightly ahead of the main exodus of students fleeing after the Marco Polo Bridge disaster, a young lecturer named Chen Boda, from "China University" in Beijing, made his way to Yan'an. Born in 1904, Chen was a decade younger than Mao, and was raised in an impoverished peasant family in Fujian province. But he later studied Marxist-Leninist philosophy in Moscow for several years and became fluent in the Russian language. Returning to China in 1931, Chen became a teacher of early Chinese history and philosophy before making his way to Yan'an. Since Chen wrote Chinese with great elegance and showed extraordinary ability to apply knowledge of dialectics to the study of the past, Mao made Chen his secretary, with responsibility for drafting his essays and speeches. Aware of Chen's ideological skills and strong Russian background, Mao also named Chen head of research in the Communist Propaganda Bureau. This was followed by an appointment at the

Yan'an central Party school, to supervise research there into Chinese problems.

Chen Boda was to become an essential ideological ally and guide to Mao. The Soviet returnees' intentions could be clearly gauged when they pushed for the rapid convocation of a Seventh Communist Party Congress in China. There had been no such assembly since the Sixth Communist Party Congress, held in Moscow in 1928. Decisions made at a new full congress would of course have power to override any further rapid and ad hoc decisions on Party leadership, such as those made at Zunyi on the Long March. Such a full congress could also prove a forum for reopening vindictive debates about Communist military policy, in which Mao had consistently argued for (and practiced when he could) a policy of guerrilla warfare in which the enemy would be lured deep into Communist-controlled terrain, forced to fragment their forces, and then attacked with overwhelming force in swift, isolated engagements. The convening of the congress was successfully (from Mao's point of view) delayed, and in July 1938 Chen Boda published the first of many articles that gave careful ideological support and justification to Mao's policies. By 1939, Chen was developing a series of intellectual arguments to show how Mao had successfully, in his writings, moved from the role of thinker and activist to the all-important sphere of "theorist." In this sense, though of course not in that of overt ideological content, Chen presented Mao's role as the new theorist of the Communist revolution as being parallel to the role of Confucius as the theorist for the "feudal" Zhou dynasty of the first millennium B.C.E. Just as Confucius caught the ideological heart of his age in his writings, said Chen, so did Mao in his Hunan report of 1927 catch the "essence" of an "entire historical period."

As Chen Boda was thus helping Mao construct an edifice of ideological dominance, Mao was also struggling with the task of keeping Yan'an a viable economic and political base. Shaanxi was very different from anyplace Mao had lived in before, and its poverty, exacerbated by the Japanese war and also by a partial Guomindang blockade of the Yan'an region, stretched Communist ingenuity to the limits. Indeed, at times the Yan'an leaders brought farmworkers into Yan'an from outlying areas to work on major irrigation projects and open up new lands, so that statistically the region could appear to be making swift strides forward. There was also the vast influx of new recruits to the Communist camp to be considered, and ideological techniques had to be devised to prove—and to develop—their loyalty.

Mao's own personal proclivities exacerbated the tensions with members of his own Party, which were never far below the surface. The cave life with He Zizhen and their baby girl, which to some outside observers seemed idyllic, had grown tense. In 1937 He Zizhen found that she was pregnant again, for the sixth time, and told Mao she wished to go to a good Shanghai hospital, to abort the fetus and also to have the shrapnel fragments removed from her body. When the Japanese occupation of Shanghai made that impossible, she decided to go to the Soviet Union instead. At the same time, she suspected that Mao was growing interested in other women. Unable to prevent her leaving—or perhaps not wanting to prevent it—Mao acquiesced in her decision to travel to the Soviet Union for medical treatment. In Moscow, she reversed her earlier decision and decided to keep the child, who was born early in 1938 but died a few months later of pneumonia. It was at this stage that Mao sent their daughter, Li Min, now two, to be with her mother in the Soviet Union. Earlier, in 1936, Mao's two

sons from his marriage to Yang Kaihui also were sent to the Soviet Union, allegedly for their safety, and for a time at least He
Zizhen looked after all three of the children. Now that she
and the children were gone, Mao set up house with a twenty-
four-year-old actress from Shandong named Jiang Qing, who
had been one of the young people who made their way to
Yan'an as the war began. Their liaison was resented by several
Communist leaders, who had liked and admired He Zizhen.
Mao and Jiang Qing had one child, a daughter named Li Na,
born in 1940. Li Na was raised in Yan'an and grew to adulthood, being the last of Mao's four surviving children from
three different women. Six of his other children died young or
disappeared.

Few people dared to criticize Mao directly for such behavior, but we can see how he was moving on a trajectory that was
pushing him more in the direction of dominance and power.
He seemed less flexible and more determined to make all those
around him conform to his own whims and beliefs. From living
the simple life because he had to, Mao had moved to choosing
to live the simple life, thence to boasting about living the
simple life, and now to forcing others to live the simple life. At
the same time, the fascination with the more complex sides of
Chinese culture that had informed Mao's youth were being re-
placed by a bitterness and irritation toward the educated people
and the aesthetic traditions in China. Part of the cause may
have come from the more highly educated students recently returned from the Soviet Union who were still trying to seize
power back from him. Or the roots may have gone back far earlier, to slights in the library at Beijing University, or to mocking
students in the Changsha normal school, when Mao was so de-
jected for a while that he even advertised for friends. Maybe
Chen Boda showed him how to use an intellectual against

an intellectual, how to open fissures and explore the wounds. Maybe he met too many people without integrity, or felt the fugitives from the big cities now arriving lacked the dignity and courage of simple country folk. Certainly the deliberate cultivation of a coarse manner was something he was now eager for visitors to see. In Yan'an, Mao flaunted his country ways, opening his belt to hunt for lice in his groin as he talked, or pulling off his trousers in the midst of an interview as he lay on the bed, to cool himself down. People began to comment on Mao's "intense and withering fury," and one young Chinese critic, braver than most, wrote of a kind of "desolation" of spirit that was beginning to spread in Yan'an, and of forces of darkness that seemed to be pushing back the light.

One thing that power brought to Mao in Yan'an was the liberty to lecture others at will, as often or as long as he liked. Perhaps that is the true obverse of honest pedagogy, of the teacher's life that Mao as a youth always said that he wanted to pursue. Nor did Mao any longer make his own detailed surveys of the countryside and its problems—he had others to do it for him, so that he could develop theory based on their results. The long years of war were indeed a triumph for the Communist Party, which emerged strengthened and more numerous, with powerfully effective techniques of mass mobilization in the rural settings and genuine skill at the manipulation of belief through well-conceptualized propaganda—something Mao had learned from his days with the Guomindang.

When Mao lectured the intellectuals now, it was on *their* own history and culture from the conceptual insights of *his* revolutionary experiences. In a lecture to inaugurate the new Yan'an Party school, given on February 1, 1942, Mao addressed the assembled cadres and intellectuals on the meaning of learning and knowledge. But his opening premise hardly encouraged frank debate: "It is a fact that the Party's General Line is correct and unquestionable," said Mao. From the Marxist-Leninist standpoint, said Mao, "a great many so-called intellectuals are actually exceedingly unlearned" and they must come to understand that "the knowledge of the workers and peasants is sometimes greater than theirs." It was a sense of humility, Mao urged, that all his educated listeners must now cultivate. They had to understand that book knowledge in and for itself was worthless, and that only words born out of the world of experience had meaning. They should never forget that "books cannot walk, and you can open and close a book at will; this is the easiest thing in the world to do, a great deal easier than it is for the cook to prepare a meal, and much easier than it is for him to slaughter a pig."

Mao was himself becoming fully confident that he knew what was "correct." The Soviet returnees and his other intellectual opponents had been almost routed, and now it was time to complete the job. In another talk to the intellectuals in May 1942, Mao offered to "exchange opinions" with his listeners, but his was the dominant voice, as he instructed the intellectuals to identify themselves fully with the proletariat and the masses rather than—as in his own youth had been his goal—to instruct and uplift them. Turning away from his youthful writings and insights, Mao spoke now against those who believed in "love" being separable from class reality, and against those questing for some kind of "love in the abstract," or those who felt "everything should proceed from love." As love was tied to class, so was "popular life" alone the "sole source" for literature and art, and the "songs sung by the masses" the true source for professional musicians. The distance from the false to the true, from the old to the new, was at once as small and as vast as the distance from the "garrets of Shanghai" to the "revolutionary base areas" that so many of the listeners had just traveled. In the months following the talk, intellectuals were divided up into small groups, where they were compelled to criticize themselves and their shortcomings, to learn to understand the past in "Maoist" terms, and to follow the correct lines in the future. Those who balked were punished. Random violence became common, and the "struggles" became deadly for many in what was euphemistically known as the "rescue campaign," supervised by Mao's growing teams of security personnel.

Mao stayed in Yan'an throughout the war, where he was sheltered from the direct force of the fighting. In the border region to the east, terrible conflicts raged, with whole swaths of countryside laid waste by the Japanese. The Communists there had to wage a constant struggle to protect the recruited peasantry from terrible reprisals. Other battles raged in the Yangtze valley, where the Communist armies were almost eliminated, not by the Japanese but by the Guomindang. When American advisory groups came to Yan'an and began to explore the possibilities of using the Communists more systematically against the Japanese, Mao was able to charm a new constituency with his earthy ways and his easy laugh. He also knew how to lobby skillfully for supplies and aid, posing his "democratic" peasant society against the landlord tyrannies of Chongqing. And always his reach and his mandate spread.

By 1943 there was emerging, in Yan'an, what can for the first time be called a "cult" of Mao. It was in May that year that Mao received two new titles that no one had held before: he was to be "chairman" of the Communist Central Committee, and chairman of the Politburo at the same time. China had now, in Mao, a true leader who "has stood the test as a strong and great revolutionary," announced the secretary-general of the Party. It could be seen that Mao stood "as the center" of all revolutionary history. In future, the people of China "should arm themselves with Comrade Mao Zedong's thought, and use Comrade Mao Zedong's system to liquidate [erroneous] thought in the Party." Every Party leader followed with similar praise—it was as if all moderating voices had been stilled. The man who had most opposed Mao at Zunyi now called him "the helmsman of the Chinese revolution." The new unanimity was matched by a concerted verbal assault on Chiang Kai-shek and any pretensions he might have to speak for China's people, a critique guided and often written by Chen Boda. In late 1943, an inner core of Mao's senior colleagues began to rewrite Chinese Party history so that Mao would be forever at the center. One by one the other rivals of the present and the past were denigrated, their "incorrect lines" exposed, and Mao's own wisdom pushed ever further back in time.

The long-delayed Seventh Party Congress met at last in Yan'an, from late April to mid-June 1945, as the war was moving to its close. Mao made a speech in which he spoke of the future for China, though he did also express regret for the violence to individual Party members, many of whom had been killed or driven to suicide. But his triumph was acknowledged in the new preamble to the Constitution of the Communist Party, presented at the congress. Totally new in all its senses and its language, it stated with absolute directness: "The Chinese Communist Party takes Mao Zedong's thought—the thought that unites Marxist-Leninist theory and the practice of the Chinese revolution—as the guide for all its work, and opposes all dogmatic or empiricist deviations." Marxism was now sinified: the leader *was* the sage.

8

Taking Over

IN THE MIDSUMMER OF 1945, no one in China guessed that the war with Japan was just about to end. Because security in Chongqing was so poor, and the Communists were politically suspect, the Chinese were not told about the American development of the atomic bomb. Besides which, even the Americans could not predict the precise effect of the atomic bombs they were to drop on Hiroshima and Nagasaki on the sixth and ninth of August, nor how soon after that the Japanese emperor would order his armies to lay down their arms, as he did on the fourteenth. Nationalists and Communists had contingency plans, of course: the Nationalists planned for a slow military advance to the east coast around Canton, spearheaded by their best American-trained divisions, to be followed by a drive north up to Shanghai and Nanjing (roughly parallel to the military advances of 1926 and 1927 in the first United Front); the Communists planned to deepen the extent of their sprawling base areas in the north, speed up land redistribution and mass mobilization, strengthen the Party organizations in the northern provinces of Shandong and Hebei, and endeavor to set up effective underground organizations in the major cities. Again, neither side could guess that Manchuria—where both Nationalists and Communists had weak or nonexistent military and political presences—would turn out to be the key to ultimate victory. When the Soviet Russian armies invaded Manchukuo on August 8, it was in response to promises they had made to Churchill and Roosevelt at Yalta that they would enter the China theater war three months after Germany's surrender— which had happened on May 8, 1945. But neither Yan'an nor Chongqing had been informed of the Yalta agreements, again for reasons of long-term strategic security.

It was a chance of geography as much as anything else that helped the Communists at this stage. From their Yan'an base, their Shanxi-Chahar-Hebei border region, and their strong guerrilla units based in Shandong province, they could move troops into Manchuria far faster than the Nationalists could, and Mao decided to take the gamble and attempt to occupy the huge region, so rich in mineral and forestry resources, though sparsely inhabited compared with the heartland of China proper. And as soon as the Communists learned of the Japanese surrender, they began to do so. They were aided considerably by the Soviet armed forces, who allowed the Chinese to take over the gigantic Japanese stockpiles of arms and ammunition in the key railroad city of Kalgan, just south of the Great Wall in Chahar. In several Inner Mongolian cities the Soviet troops first subdued and disarmed the Japanese, and then retreated, allowing the Chinese to come in unopposed. In some areas the Russians gave Japanese arms and vehicles directly to the Chinese, and in at least one case, the Russians and Chinese fought side by side to seize a key border city. Russian logistical help was equally great, with as many as 100,000 Chinese Communist troops and 50,000 political workers being ferried into southern Manchuria from Shandong and northern Jiangsu provinces, and these forces were able to seize and hold several major cities.

From figures released later in Moscow it is possible to

calculate the arms the Russians made available to the Communists at this time, and they totaled around 740,000 rifles, 18,000 machine guns, 800 aircraft, and 4,000 artillery pieces. This was roughly the same as the entire total that the Nationalist armies were able to seize from the Japanese inside China proper. The Soviet help took place, also, in the face of a massive air- and sea-lift of Nationalist troops to the north by the United States, which was anxious to prevent a Communist resurgence. Two divisions of U.S. Marines, totaling 53,000 men in all, were deployed on the north China coast by the end of September 1945, and in addition Japanese troops were left armed and in position at many points to prevent Communist takeovers.

Mao showed considerable personal courage, and a certain willingness to negotiate, by agreeing to accompany the American ambassador, Patrick Hurley, on a trip to Chongqing in late August, where he stayed until October. This must have been Mao's first sight of Chiang Kai-shek since 1926 in Canton, on the eve of the northern expedition. The two men agreed to form a unified national army, though the date was left unspecified, and Mao agreed to pull any remaining Communist forces back from south China. The two sides also moved to reconvene the joint deliberative body known as the "Political Consultative Conference," so as to discuss China's long-range future.

But there was little substantive effort to halt the escalating hostilities, and in a special report issued in December 1945, Mao outlined a general strategy for the occupation of all of Manchuria except the south during the year 1946, though he noted it would be a "hard and bitter struggle." He thought rural base areas should be established across Manchuria, though away from major cities and communications routes, to stop possible Guomindang attacks. Mass ideological work would take place as a fundamental part of increasing the Party's basic military strength. Land reform should be moderate initially, to develop a wide basis of support—limited to "struggles to settle accounts with traitors," and to some campaigns "for rent-reduction and wage increases." The Communists must at all costs bring "tangible material benefits to the people in the northeast," who otherwise might "be taken in for a time by deceitful Guomindang propaganda, and may even turn against our party." But Mao was firm about keeping options open in the rest of China. When General George Marshall came to China to speed negotiations, on President Truman's orders, and when the Political Consultative Conference did in fact meet that same year, Mao warned his comrades not to let their hatred of the Guomindang push them to reject all chance of peaceful settlement: that would be "narrow closed-doorism."

Fighting became fierce in Manchuria after the Marshall peace talks broke down, and the Communists lost several areas they had controlled in the southern part of the region; but they held on firmly in the north and successfully carried out their program of setting up isolated base areas with mass support, pursuing moderate land reform, and strengthening their military units. In north China, however, land reform in the areas the Communists controlled became increasingly violent, with mass killings of landlords, total seizures of their land and property, and redistribution of land on an egalitarian basis to all peasants and their family members. This "extremism" was widely debated by the Party leaders, but not effectively checked. At the same time, any incidents that could be used among the Chinese as a whole to strengthen the negative perceptions of the Guomindang and their American helpers were skillfully followed up by the pro-Communist propaganda organs. The murder of one of China's most celebrated poets, Wen Yiduo, a great writer and scholar, was one such example. During the war, Wen had lived in Kunming, at the associated university, and had been a vocal critic of Chiang Kai-shek. His assassination was nationally attributed to Guomindang secret agents, for Wen had just given a passionate speech on behalf of a friend of his—also murdered for political reasons—when he himself was gunned down. And in Beijing, the rape by two American servicemen of a Chinese student returning from a nighttime movie, and clumsy government attempts to cover up the incident, were exploited in newspapers and at huge student rallies, to underline the Communist cause. The raped woman was presented as representative of a victimized China, helpless in the arms of aggressive capitalist and imperialist forces.

Despite their difficulties in Manchuria, the Nationalist armies were able to surround and eventually capture Yan'an in March 1947. This was a major symbolic victory, but no more than that, for most of the Communist forces, and all their major leaders still in the region, withdrew in good time and moved to new bases farther to the north. At this point, Mao was with Jiang Qing and their daughter, Li Na, and spent some of the time with his oldest son by Yang Kaihui, Mao Anying, now aged twenty-four, who had returned from the Soviet Union in 1946 and joined his father in Yan'an. Anying was courting a young woman he met in Yan'an whose father had been killed by warlords, as Anying's mother had been. They married in 1949. Mao's second son, Anqing, returned home, too, but to Harbin, where he arrived in 1947. He Zizhen also returned in 1947, with her daughter, Li Min; she did not see Mao at this time, and later made her own way to Shanghai.

It was from his northern retreat in Shaanxi, in September 1947, that Mao issued what came to be seen as one of his most important pronouncements on military strategy. He wrote in the context of the struggle in China as it was being waged at that time, with the idea of tracing essential military principles. He had already decided, within a week of Hiroshima, that the atomic bomb was not the crucial factor in ending the war with Japan that some people held it to be, and in August 1946 he told an American journalist that he considered the atomic bomb a "paper tiger," looking more terrible than in fact it was. In his September 1947 statement, Mao announced that the Communist armies were now ready to launch a "nationwide counteroffensive," to seize the initiative away from the Guomindang by moving from the "interior lines" of warfare to the "exterior lines." Each time they smashed their way into a former Guomindang area, the Communists would set up bases there, from which in turn they would launch new campaigns. Despite the need for such base areas, destroying the enemy and capturing their weapons always took precedence over "holding and seizing a place." Mao's maxims were simple but by this time were the fruit of long experience: "Be sure to fight no battle unprepared, fight no battle you are not sure of winning," and fight relentlessly, giving the enemy no time to recoup. Use at once all the arms and at least 80 to 90 percent of all captured troops (though not their officers); take supplies from the Guomindang-dominated areas, not from older Communist base areas; carry out land reform in both old and newly liberated areas.

The strategy was astonishingly successful. By the following year Communist troops had totally routed the Guomindang armies in Manchuria and were ready to move south. As

Guomindang military morale collapsed, accompanied by civilian revulsion with the financial chaos caused by rampant inflation, and the continued harsh repression of all dissent, the Communists consolidated their gains and advanced with incredible rapidity, entering Beijing in January 1949, Nanjing in April, Shanghai in May, and Changsha in August. With Canton encircled, though not yet captured, on October 1, 1949, Mao and the senior leaders of the Communist Party then in the region of Beijing climbed to a reviewing stand on the Great Tiananmen gate, at the south of the Forbidden City; there, in front of a small bank of microphones, as a few planes of the Chinese air force circled overhead, Mao announced the formation of the People's Republic of China.

Within weeks, Mao was planning a visit to the Soviet Union so that he could confer in person with the man who in so many ways had been his inspiration but also almost his nemesis, Joseph Stalin. When Mao set off for Moscow in December 1949, the Communists had won, but China was in a catastrophic state. Many areas of the country had endured close to forty years of almost incessant fighting or military occupation of one kind or another—local warlords, Communist guerrillas, Guomindang suppression forces, Japanese occupying armies—and had no effective administrative structures. The economy was in a shambles, there was no stable or unified currency, inflation was out of control, and communications networks were in disarray, with rail tracks destroyed and rivers and harbors clogged with sunken ships. Millions of people had been displaced by the wars, and the Communists' own armies were bloated by hundreds of thousands of Nationalist soldiers who had been admitted to their ranks with virtually no scrutiny. Schools and universities had decaying buildings, few books, and many ineffective teachers whose only qualification had been political loyalty to the Guomindang. The hunt for Japanese collaborators had soured personal relations, and the carpetbagging nature of the Guomindang reoccupation of the formerly Japanese-occupied cities had been accompanied by corruption, looting, reprisals, and theft of assets.

On the borders, the situation was little better. To the far west, in Xinjiang, the Muslim population had fought for many years to gain autonomy from China, and the local warlord had shifted erratically between overreliance on the Soviet Union and uneasy alliance with the Guomindang. Mao Zedong's last surviving sibling, his younger brother Mao Zemin, had been executed there as part of these political machinations, in 1943. Mongolia had become an independent republic, but was totally dominated by the Soviet Union. Tibet had also achieved considerable levels of autonomy in the 1930s and 1940s—in his own youthful writings Mao had regularly called for autonomy and self-rule for Mongols, Tibetans, and Muslims—and the Chinese now had to decide whether to launch an invasion or allow Tibetan independence to grow, under the young and ambitious new Dalai Lama. The French were re-strengthening their colonial empire in Southeast Asia, and though both they and the British had been forced to give up their concession areas in Shanghai during 1943, the British had reasserted their control over Hong Kong in 1945—with Guomindang acquiescence—and once more ruled it as a colony. Taiwan had been chosen by Chiang Kai-shek as the temporary base for his administration and his armies, pending his planned return to the mainland. It was strongly defended, and it would take a massive air- and seaborne assault to bring it into the Communist camp.

From the Russian transcripts of the personal talks between Mao and Stalin, preserved in Moscow, we are able to see—free of any possible Chinese re-editing—how the two world leaders of the Communists related to each other. Stalin must have been an intensely formidable figure to Mao—he was a founding father of the Soviet Revolution, a former close associate of Lenin's, the builder of the autocratic central power and police apparatus of the Soviet Union, the guide and inspiration to his people in the terrible years of the German invasion, and the architect of postwar Soviet expansion into Eastern Europe. His voluminous historical and analytical works were required reading for all Communists and fellow travelers—Mao, among countless other Chinese, had studied them in Yan'an, and tried to come to grips with many of their arguments in an attempt to gauge their relevance to China. To Stalin, Mao was an unknown entity, tenacious but self-educated and undisciplined, a pursuer of political lines that often ran in direct opposition to stated Soviet policies. But Mao had won against great odds, and that certainly commanded respect, as did the fact that he was now in control of the world's second-largest—and most populous—Communist state.

Their first meeting was on December 16, 1949. After opening pleasantries, Mao observed to Stalin that what China needed was "three to five years of peace," so as to "bring the economy back to pre-war levels, and stabilize the country in general." Given this priority for China, Mao ventured to ask the Soviet leader what he thought of the chances for the preservation of peace internationally. Stalin's reply was bland and elliptical: China wanted peace, Japan was not ready for another war, the United States was "afraid" of further war, as were the Europeans. Thus no one would fight the Chinese, unless the North Korean Kim Il Sung decided to invade China.

On the question of the Sino-Soviet treaty of 1945, which Stalin had signed with Chiang Kai-shek, both Mao and Stalin reached tacit agreement: the treaty would be allowed to stand for now, so as not to give any grounds to the British and Americans for modifying any of their own agreements with the Soviet Union. But the Russians would withdraw their troops from Port Arthur when the Chinese wished, and also yield up control of the trans-Manchurian railways. On other practical matters, Mao requested Soviet credits of 300 million U.S. dollars, as well as help developing domestic air transport routes and developing a navy, to all of which Stalin agreed. But when Mao asked for Soviet help in conquering Taiwan—specifically, "volunteer pilots or secret military detachments"—Stalin stalled, offering "headquarters staff and instructors" instead, and suggesting that Mao send his own propaganda forces to Taiwan to foment an insurrection. On the question of Hong Kong, Stalin ingeniously and deviously suggested that Mao encourage conflicts between Guangdong province and the British colony, and then step forward as "mediator" to resolve them, thus presumably increasing his international status as a statesman. Foreign business enterprises in China and foreign-run schools, both men agreed, should be carefully monitored. China should speed up its extraction of rare minerals—Stalin specifically mentioned tungsten and molybdenum—and build oil pipelines. Mao again reiterated that he needed to know the long-range prospects for peace if he was to undertake such projects, since it was on the chances for peace that hinged such key decisions as whether to concentrate on developing China's coastal industry, or to move the industrial development to sites inland.

The final part of their talk hinged on Maoist ideology, and suggests that Stalin was fully aware of the claims to be a theoretical leader that Mao had been steadily developing since 1937. Stalin broached the subject abruptly by asking for a list of Mao's works that Mao felt should be translated into Russian. Mao, apparently unprepared for the question, stalled. "I am currently reviewing my works which were published in various local publishing houses," he countered, for they "contain a mass of errors and misrepresentations. I plan to complete this review by spring of 1950." Mao wanted Soviet help, he continued, not only with the Russian translation, but also "in editing the Chinese original." Now it was Stalin's turn to be surprised: "You need your works edited?" "Yes," Mao replied. "It can be arranged," responded Stalin, "if indeed there is such a need."

At this December 1949 meeting, Mao was the only Chinese present except for his own interpreter, so he had only his wits to rely on. At the subsequent meeting with Stalin on January 22, 1950—the only other one Mao ever had—a small but high-powered Chinese delegation was with Mao, which included Zhou Enlai and Chen Boda, Mao's ideological assistant from Yan'an. Along with a stream of polemical and historical works, Chen had just published a book on Stalin's contributions to the Chinese Revolution. Clearly his presence in Moscow was partly to reassure Mao about ideological matters if the going got difficult, but also perhaps to temper Mao's exuberance and make sure that he did not go out on any limbs that might later upset his powerful colleagues back in China. In the presence of such a delegation, the discussion remained at a technical level, about details of aid, its nature, and the interest to be paid. The most frank exchange was over Tibet. Mao asked Stalin directly to continue the loan of a Soviet air regiment to China, which had already helped move more than 10,000 troops inside China; the regiment was needed, said Mao, to help transport provisions to the Chinese troops "currently preparing for an attack on Tibet." "It's good that you are preparing to attack. The Tibetans need to be subdued," was Stalin's reply, though he added that he would have to talk the matter over with his military experts.

While various negotiators stayed in Moscow to iron out the details of the "Sino-Soviet treaty of friendship," Mao returned home to oversee the reconstruction of the country. In his blunt way, Stalin had told Mao directly that the Soviets assumed "the Chinese economy was practically in ruins." Mao had not disagreed. In 1950, the Communist leaders confronted the immense task of planning a politically stable and economically viable regime. Among the tactics used were the crash-training of students and young Party members in the principles of land reform, and their dispatch across China to implement and oversee a program of land redistribution; the establishment of a countrywide government structure, subdivided by regions, each of which would be supervised by a combine of Party ideologues, civil bureaucrats, and military personnel; the development of a new group of ministries in Beijing, with their staffs, to oversee national defense and industrial development; the state supervision and reconstruction of the school and college system, along with a state-controlled system of newspapers, journals, and radio broadcasts to induce ideological consistency and obedience; a program of railroad repair and expansion; the initial planning for state ownership of the larger industrial plants, and the concomitant negotiations with their domestic or foreign owners; and the disarming of the civilian population and the hunting down of alleged "counterrevolutionaries."

On other moral fronts the Party leadership moved with comparable energy: brothels were forced to register, prior to their phased closures, and the prostitutes were sent to special training schools for "reeducation"; drug addicts were also ordered to register with the state authorities and to undergo phased rehabilitation programs under state and family supervision, while opium poppy–growing was checked and distributors of drugs were imprisoned or executed. In terms of the preservation of the old China, Mao made one fateful decision. In late 1948, on the eve of the attack on Beijing, Communist artillery commanders had asked for—and obtained—lists of national treasures in the city, so that, if possible, they would not be destroyed by artillery fire. This seemed a good omen to preservationists and art historians, one of whom presented to the Communist leadership a master plan to create the world's most beautiful system of parks, to run along the tops of the immense and beautiful systems of old walls that encircled the city of Beijing. These parks would be combined with the designation of old Beijing as an industry-free zone, the construction of a new industrial quarter farther out in the countryside, and the building of an entirely new administrative city to house the personnel of the swiftly growing Communist bureaucracy. Mao vetoed the plan, suggesting with a sweep of his arms across the old city that he would rather see it lined from end to end with smokestacks as a symbol of China's economic rejuvenation. So, over the following years, with the single exception of the Forbidden City palace itself, Beijing's entire system of magnificent walls and gates was destroyed to create ring roads for the city; industry grew rapidly within the city itself; and the area south of the Forbidden City—which remained, as it had been under the Republic, a museum for the people—was leveled to make a colossal square in which a million people could assemble for political rallies, and which was bordered by the huge block-like assembly halls and bureaus of the new government.

Mao, along with the other senior Communist Party leaders, moved into the old walled complex of buildings adjacent to the southwest corner of the Forbidden City, nestled around the ornamental South Lake and bordering on the North Lake park where he had courted Yang Kaihui thirty years before. In this sheltered and closely guarded area, known as Zhongnanhai, he and Jiang Qing made their home, establishing the first general semblance of a conventional family life that Mao had known since perhaps 1923. Here he had a chance to swim once again—a covered pool was soon built, so he could pursue his favorite form of exercise—and to read with his two daughters, Li Min and Li Na, who were enrolled at a nearby school. His elder son, Anying, was married and working in a Beijing machinery plant, though he and his wife had not yet had children. The younger son, Anqing, who had never been fully well since his dark days in Shanghai, was sometimes hospitalized for treatment, and had not yet married. Once a week, in the evening, there was dancing, to the nostalgic sounds of old Western foxtrots and waltzes, along with occasional film shows. Mao got his books together in one place and read widely.

With so many things of such importance to be done, it is almost inconceivable to imagine that Mao wanted the Korean War. He had specifically asked Stalin about the chances for long-range peace at their December 1949 meetings, and at the January meeting he urged Stalin to always have "consultation regarding international concerns" with China. In retrospect, we can see that Stalin lied to Mao, for Stalin was already secretly discussing the plans for an invasion of the South with North

Korea's leader, Kim Il Sung. And yet, we know that by March 1950 Mao was alerted to the possibility of a North Korean attack on the South, and that he told the North Korean ambassador in Beijing that he encouraged such an attack, and that the Chinese might even intervene to help North Korea. Mao's estimate of the military situation was colored by his own experiences of people's war, and the effectiveness of his lightly trained and equipped guerrilla peasant forces against the Japanese. Mao, who had already declared the atomic bomb a paper tiger, had at first told the Koreans that he was sure the Americans would not intervene. When they did so, in late June, right after the North Korean attack, Mao shared with many of the Communist commanders a sense that the Americans were not politically motivated and were too tightly bound by their military codes and regulations, so that "their tactics are dull and mechanical." Americans were also "afraid of dying" and were over-reliant on firepower. By contrast, Chinese troops were tactically flexible and politically conscious, needed little equipment, "and are good at close combat, night battles, mountainous assaults, and bayonet charges."

Although contingency plans were made to send in large numbers of Chinese troops under the guise of volunteers, all through the summer and fall the Chinese troops did not enter Korea. Mao was locked in an intense debate with his senior colleagues and military commanders over which was the best course to follow. His colleagues wanted guarantees of Soviet air support and supplies of Soviet vehicles, weapons, and ammunition; some of them also pointed out that the war would wipe out China's economic reconstruction, and the Chinese people would grow disaffected. They also pointed to the gross disparities in industrial potential. The previous year China had produced 610,000 tons of iron and steel; the United States produced 87.7 million tons in the same period. Lin Biao, the victorious coordinating commander of the Manchurian campaigns two years before, pointed out that the narrow Korean peninsula was particularly bad ground for the Chinese to choose, since they had neither air- nor seapower. Mao's argument that China *had* to intervene, to secure its own borders as well as to save its neighboring Communist ally, reinforced by his own optimism concerning the Chinese soldiers' potential, finally triumphed over his advisers' misgivings. After further delays—this time by Stalin, who agreed to use Soviet planes only to protect China's coastal defenses, not in Korean combat, and who hesitated over the amount of supplies to be made available—the Chinese "volunteers" finally began to enter Korea on the night of October 19, under the command of the veteran Communist general Peng Dehuai, maintaining total radio silence, using no lights on their vehicles, and with advance units dressed in the uniforms of North Korean troops.

An early casualty of the war was Mao's recently married oldest son, Mao Anying, age twenty-eight. Unlike most of the Chinese combat troops, he was indeed a "volunteer," whose service in Korea Mao had agreed to. Anying had requested an infantry command position, but fearing for the young man's safety, General Peng Dehaui assigned him to headquarters, as staff officer and Russian interpreter. Mao Anying's position was hit by a U.S./U.N. incendiary bomb during an attack on November 24, 1950, and he was killed. At first no one dared to tell his father, and his body was buried in North Korea like any other Chinese casualty. When Mao was finally told of his son's death by Peng Dehuai in person, he agreed to let the body remain in Korean soil, as an example of duty to the Chinese people. His two recorded public pronouncements on his loss were brief: "In war there must be sacrifice. Without sacrifice there will be no victory. There are no parents in the world who do not treasure their children." And again, "We understand the hows and whys of these things. There are so many common folk whose children have shed their blood and were sacrificed for the sake of the revolution."

For the whole early part of the war, while the fighting was heaviest, Mao followed the campaigns with meticulous attention, intervening countless times with his own orders or tactical suggestions. But at the same time, with his acute sense of effective propaganda, he saw the advantages of the war as a political rallying cry inside China itself. Aware for so many years of the intense emotional and political fervor that could be generated among workers, students, or peasants by skillfully orchestrated campaigns, Mao and the Chinese propaganda organs spread the word through massive "Aid Korea, Resist America" campaigns. The Chinese people were called upon to sacrifice more, to impose greater vigilance on themselves and their communities, to pledge themselves in deeper loyalty to the Communist Party. As the Korean War entered a protracted stalemate period that lasted until 1953, the domestic campaigns were extended to include all-out hunts for domestic counterrevolutionaries and foreign spies, and they began to target capitalists or corrupt bureaucrats. Mao himself, as instigator and manipulator of the war on Korean soil, slowly began to assume the same total roles in his supervision of the Chinese people. Though such campaigns were focused on individuals, they also had an abstracted quality, a certain tokenism and quota-meeting aspect that promised harmony for the majority if the correct percentage of victims could be found. In such an aura of fear, it was hard to keep one's sense of moral balance. Mao was still surrounded by powerful, intelligent, and experienced revolutionary colleagues, but it was becoming ever harder for them to cut through the protective coating with which he was encasing his inner, visionary worlds.

The Ultimate Vision

As soon as the Korean War ended with the Treaty of 1953—
which left the dividing lines between the two halves of the
country close to where they had been before the war began—
China embarked on an ambitious program of coordinated national reconstruction. The Communist leaders modeled their
scenario along the lines of the Soviet Union's Five-Year Plans,
with the goal of giving maximum growth to industrial development, especially steel production and mining, with secondary
growth planned for consumer goods and the agricultural sector. Compulsory purchases of grain from peasants at below market price would help fuel the industrial growth, and at the same
time enable the government to subsidize the food prices in the
larger cities to prevent major unrest there. Workers in state-
controlled industries had what was termed an "iron rice bowl":
they were almost never fired, not even for poor performance or
tardiness, and the state provided a massive safety net for them
through cheap subsidized housing, free medical care, and access to schools. Thus, though incomes were low, the standard
of living was adequate for most workers, and their "work unit"
became the source of their social and economic identity.

Mao knew the countryside better than he knew the cities,
and hence it is not surprising that peasants had a more varied

range of economic options than urban workers, depending on their wealth before 1949 and on the amount of land they might have received through land redistribution. Ever since the Jiangxi Soviet days, but especially since the mass-mobilization periods of World War II, Maoist ideology had made "class labeling" a central factor in peasants' lives. To be labeled a rich peasant or landlord was to face the risk of losing everything, including all one's savings and even one's life. To be labeled a middle peasant was of marginal danger, and might well subject one to mass criticism and partial confiscation of property. To be classified as a poor peasant or landless laborer was the safest. The exact way that these labels were applied, and the precise amount of land or other property, tools, and draft animals that each individual or family controlled, were drawn up in exhaustive investigations, a prototype of which had been the kinds of investigations carried out by Mao in Hunan during 1926, in Jinggangshan in 1928, and in Xunwu in 1930. Facing such investigations, wealthy peasants often sought to "lower" their class status by killing off livestock or destroying stored grain, and by selling off cheaply, or even giving away, surplus land. There was much settling of old scores in this process, along with great social violence, often exacerbated by struggles between formerly married couples once the Communists' liberal divorce laws became effective in 1950.

Sometimes the inequities were patent, as with the case of poor peasants who had joined in various types of cooperative organizations at the urging of the Party during the civil war period, and had done well enough out of the new socialist organization to be later classified as middle peasants. In the early 1950s, great areas of the countryside were still desperately poor, and private ownership of land, even after redistribution, was still the norm. The preferred form of socialism was through low-level producers' cooperatives, in which some labor, land, and draft animals would be pooled, and peasants would withdraw in income amounts commensurate with their original input. An effective registration system tied peasants to the area where they worked the land, transposing the former rural village organizations into "work units." In an attempt to prevent a flood of migrant laborers from the poorer areas of countryside into the cities, the Communist Party only in exceptional circumstances granted permission to travel away from the work unit. Under this system many hardworking peasants indubitably got richer, while others were pushed to the margins of subsistence.

As the recognized leader of the new China, presiding over close to 600 million people and an immense stratified bureaucracy, Mao was forced to spend much of his energies on national planning. Yet at the same time, from the preserved files of Mao's correspondence in the early 1950s it is possible to see how news reached him across space and decades from three groups of people that he had known at a much more intimate level: the family of his previous wife, Yang Kaihui; the residents of his native village of Shaoshan or the adjacent market town of Xiangtan; and those who taught Mao or studied with him in Changsha. These letters gave him an intimate view of how the revolution was affecting individuals he knew well, and enabled him to place the larger national criteria in a smaller-scale series of contexts.

The Yang family were quickest off the mark. The first of their letters reached Mao just a week after he formally announced, from his rostrum atop Tiananmen, the formation of the People's Republic of China. It came from Yang Kaihui's brother, Yang Kaizhi. Kaizhi asked permission to come to the capital with some of his relatives. His mother—Mao's previous mother-in-law—was not well, and she needed assistance. Kaizhi also wanted a job. In a frank but courteous reply, Mao told his brother-in-law not to come to the capital and not to put Mao "on the spot" by requesting special favors. Let the Hunan provincial committee of the Communist Party find him appropriate employment.

But the mere fact that Mao replied at all gave the Yang family recipients prestige and a major lift in their communities. By the following April, Yang Kaizhi could report that he was working for the provincial government of Hunan. An uncle of Yang Kaihui's also wrote to Mao and received a courteous if guarded reply. Mao was more forthcoming when he got a letter from Li Shuyi, Yang Kaihui's closest girlhood friend in the Fuxiang girls' school of Changsha. Li Shuyi's husband, a close boyhood friend of Mao's, had been shot by the same warlord who killed Yang Kaihui, giving the two surviving spouses an unusual kind of bond from the old days, which they relived by sharing poems. Li Shuyi desired to come to Beijing so that she could "study Marxism-Leninism with greater seriousness." Mao dissuaded her from coming, but she later wrote again, asking Mao to help her get a job at the Beijing Literature and History Museum. Mao demurred, but offered to help her with some of the money he made from his publishing income. Presumably he was being well paid for his "Selected Works."

A different voice from the intimate past was that of the nanny, Chen Yuying, whom Mao and Yang Kaihui had hired to look after their three children in the late 1920s. Writing on December 18, 1951, she reminded Mao of her loyalty to his children and requested permission to come and visit him. He gently deflected her, using "thrift" as his reason. She should stay in Changsha and work there, but if she needed assistance, Mao would try to see that she received it. Other letters show that Mao was sending, through his personal secretary, two payments every year to the Yang family as a "subsidy." The payments were large, each one being at least ten times more than a well-off peasant's annual income at that time. Mao also arranged for visits to the Yang family graves, and for special celebrations in honor of Yang Kaihui's mother, who was still alive in the early 1950s.

Other correspondents, evoking Mao's past, had stranger tales to tell. One classmate of Mao's from the Changsha normal school had gone on to become an assemblyman under the Beijing militarists and later a member of the Guomindang. Now he was in financial straits. Mao arranged for him to be given some help. Another schoolmate of Mao's from an even earlier time, when they attended the Xiangxiang primary school, reported that his two sons had been shot as counterrevolutionaries during the land reform of 1952. Because of his children's crimes, the father was put under surveillance for a year and forbidden membership in the local peasant association. *His* only crime was to have worked for the Guomindang for five months in 1928. He now claimed poor-peasant status. Mao suggested he continue to reform and "listen to the cadres."

Pushing Mao's memories back to the fall of the Qing dynasty, two of Mao's Changsha normal-school teachers wrote, one a former principal and the other a history instructor. Now in their seventies, both were in dire financial need. They also reported that Mao's revered classical literature teacher, "Yuan the Beard," had died, leaving his seventy-year-old widow starving. Mao suggested a small subsidy from local Party funds for all three. The daughter-in-law of Mao's math teacher from the same school (he had hated mathematics) wrote, trying to get three (of her eight) children into a school for Communist cadre relatives. Mao was not sure it would be possible, but he gave her some names to try and said she could use his reply letter to vouch for her. A spate of other letters came from army men he knew in 1911, Shaoshan and Xiangtan residents, staff of the 1919 magazine *New Hunan*, and members of the New People's Study Society, of which Mao had been the diligent secretary in 1920. Some of these pointed out grave local abuses in the way the Party was now operating, especially in grain requisitioning and bandit suppression.

But such personal village and family voices tailed off as Mao's obligations increased. By late 1953, when he celebrated his sixtieth birthday, Mao was not only chairman of the Communist Party, which now had more than five million members, and chairman of the military commission that controlled the armed forces, he was also chairman of the People's Republic of China itself. In addition to the maze of the ministries in Beijing—there were already thirty-five, and the number was soon to double—the Party had its own organization in every province and rural township, while the military were subdivided into regional zones, each of which had to integrate its operations with the administrative and Party structures. The small Standing Committee of the Politburo, over which Mao presided, thus had to supervise the ultimate integration of all these sub-units. With all these demands on Mao's time, the growing array of private secretaries and bureaucrats around him began to process and sort his letters for him, and those that criticized the government or the Party were often returned—without Mao's knowledge—to the very local leaders who were being criticized. Furthermore, the end of the Korean War and Stalin's death in 1953 left Mao in a virtually unchallengeable position within the world Communist pantheon. Mao's "thought" was specified as being the inspiration for the country's economic growth and political energies. Yet at the same time Mao himself often felt isolated from events, as expert organizers like Zhou Enlai and Liu Shaoqi coordinated the multifaceted layers of foreign and economic policy.

In 1953 and 1954 Mao used his personal prestige to purge two of the formerly most powerful Party political bosses, one in Manchuria and one in Shanghai, whom he suspected of being disloyal to his overall revolutionary goals. In 1955, he began to call for sharper levels of radical reorganization in the country-side and for the formation of larger cooperative units, in which more of the land would be worked in common by peasants and the use of private plots and informal markets would be strictly limited. This so-called Little Leap was intended to generate more income for the industrial sector, as well as to tighten the revolutionary fervor of the people. The cooperative idea was paralleled by the mass mobilizations of tens of thousands (some-times hundreds of thousands) of rural workers to undertake ma-jor projects such as reservoir building or digging canals and terracing hillsides. Such projects were customarily hailed in the state-controlled press as proof of the "higher stage" of socialist organization, and if they were not given intensive coverage Mao suspected disloyalty on the part of the editorial staff.

These huge ventures were either orchestrated by Mao in person or implemented by local Party leaders who sought thus to ingratiate themselves with the "chairman," as Mao was now generally addressed. But many senior leaders in the Party found these methods ideologically distasteful and economically un-sound. They felt that the bulk of rural wealth was generated by the ablest and hardest-working rich peasants, who therefore should be encouraged to increase their holdings and their crop harvests, so that the state could extract the surplus for the industrial sector. In a forceful speech of July 1955, Mao struck back at such theorists: "An upsurge in the new, Socialist mass movement is imminent throughout the countryside. But some of our comrades, tottering along like a woman with bound feet, are complaining all the time, 'You're going too fast, much too fast.' " Of course there were minor problems, said Mao: sometimes poor peasants were kept out of co-ops despite their poverty; sometimes middle peasants were forced into cooperatives against their interests. Also, though there were around 650,000 cooperatives in China, containing a total of 16,900,000 peasants, they averaged out at only about twenty-six households in each, and tended to be bunched in north China. Unless they could be consolidated in larger units and spread more widely, rapid growth was out of the question. This expanding co-op movement, Mao believed, had two distinct kinds of problems. One was overoptimism, which caused cadres and peasants to be "dizzy with success." This could be considered a "leftist deviation." The other was to be "scared of success" and eager to cut back the movement. That was a "rightist deviation," and was currently the main problem.

The phrase "dizzy with success" in such an agrarian context was drawn from the works of Stalin, as Mao's listeners would have known well. It referred to the early stages of Soviet collectivization, when many officials moved too fast, alienating millions of farmers and causing widespread suffering. Yes, said Mao, there had been "impetuosity and rashness" in the Soviet Union, but "on no account should we allow these comrades to use the Soviet experience as a cover for their idea of moving at a snail's pace." In many rural areas in the Soviet Union there had been inadequate preparatory work, and the peasants were not at a high level of political consciousness. China was already rectifying both areas, and Mao intended the full plan to implement "socialist cooperative agriculture" to take eighteen years in all, from the founding of the People's Republic in 1949 to the end of the Third Five-Year Plan, in 1967–68.

Mao had already, in fact, decided to move considerably faster than that, but before he did so, he had to woo over foot-draggers in the Party, and also be sure of the enthusiastic support of the writers and intellectuals who fueled the Party's propaganda campaigns and educational work. The situation was complicated by Nikita Khrushchev, First Secretary of the Communist Party of the U.S.S.R., whose totally unexpected denunciation of Stalin in 1956, in a speech that not only denigrated the Soviet Union's core leader, in Mao's eyes, but also by implication criticized Mao himself, for his "cult of personality" was by this time well orchestrated and perfectly obvious to any informed outside observers.

Ever since the Yan'an days, Mao had been determined to play a leading role as a cultural critic and arbiter. After 1949, Mao often intervened in discussions on film, literature, and philosophy to emphasize the need for vigilance in rooting out negative aspects of the old society, and he supported ordinary people, whom he sardonically referred to as "the nobodies," whenever they had the courage to attack well-known artistic works in the name of revolutionary purity.

In late 1956 and early 1957 these various tracks converged in Mao's mind: the ability of the nobodies of China to transform their society, the obstructionism of the Communist Party's own new establishment, the possibilities of vast economic strides forward if those with "bound feet" would get out of the way, the need to deepen the channels of criticism and the flow of information and to keep the brightest flames of socialism burning. All of these played a part both in the outpouring of criticism during the middle of 1957, and the launching of the Great Leap Forward in industry and agriculture later that year.

A long text by Mao gives a sense of his thinking in February 1957. These are the rough notes to an informal four-hour speech that Mao gave in a rather formal setting—that of the Supreme State Conference, attended by leaders of the bureaucracy, the cultural and propaganda spheres, and selected non-Party intellectuals.

The topic of the speech was "contradictions," within Chinese society and within the Party, and this evoked the theme that Mao had first broached in his earliest attempts to have himself seen as an expert in Marxist dialectical materialism back in 1937. "Contradictions," to Mao, were of two kinds, those between "the enemy and ourselves," which were to be called "antagonistic," and those "among the people," which were "non-antagonistic." The "enemy," in the Chinese context, would include landlords, "imperialist elements" (presumably those with foreign connections), and the Chinese refugees in Taiwan. Such people were correctly deprived of their civil rights under people's dictatorship and democratic centralism. This was what constituted Chinese democracy: it was "democracy with leadership," or "class freedom," more genuine in China than the bourgeois "facade" of parliamentary freedom in the West. But though the logic of class war would suggest that the Chinese national bourgeoisie would also be the enemy of the Chinese working class, that was not in fact so. "Antagonistic contradictions, if properly handled, can become unantagonistic," and that was just what happened in China due to the joint struggle against foreign imperialism. Care was needed in defining enemies and working out when to exercise compassion, or to decide when transformation was completed. "The American moon and the Chinese moon are the same moon," noted Mao; the American moon was not *better*. In other words, each society looks up to the sky from its own class vantage point.

Mao had decided that the process of unity-criticism-unity should be seen as the correct way to resolve contradictions among the people or contradictions within the Communist Party itself. Such a method was better than the "ruthless struggle and merciless blows" approach used by Stalin, for Mao now felt that when Stalin was in power, he often "did things badly." The Seventh Party Congress of 1945 was an example of the correct process at work. Looking at the Chinese counter-revolutionaries who had been killed—according to Mao, some 700,000 "local bullies and evil gentry" between 1950 and 1952—one saw there were no errors. All of them deserved to die. But when Hong Kong papers claimed twenty million had died they were obviously wide of the mark. "How could we possibly kill twenty million people?" Mao asked.

Throughout his talk, Mao inserted the kinds of statistics that he had loved to gather in his youth. Though impressionistic, they reveal the sense he had of China's continuing problems: the dissatisfaction rate of peasants with the co-ops was 2 to 5 percent; households lacking adequate food constituted 10 to 15 percent of the population; 40 percent of children in China had no schools to go to; state grain procurement was around 22 percent of the total produced; 7,000 students in twenty-nine schools demonstrated against the government during 1956; labor unions launched at least fifty strikes, some involving over a thousand workers. In such circumstances, why not "let a hundred flowers bloom, and a hundred schools of thought contend"? That would be an excellent aid to socialist transformation. As for the leaders, being misunderstood in one's own time was no bad thing, said Mao: it had happened to Jesus and to Confucius, to Sakyamuni Buddha and to Charles Darwin, to Martin Luther and to Galileo.

This curious speech did indeed encourage intellectuals and critics to speak out with great frankness that summer in the spirit of "a hundred flowers," just as the seeds Mao had sown in terms of adventurousness in agricultural policy were to germinate later in the year into the Great Leap Forward. Each was followed—as indeed dialectical thinking might have forewarned Mao—by its total negation. The intellectuals who spoke out boldly against abuses in the Party bureaucracy, against pointless constraints on creativity, and even against the relevance of Marxism itself to China's needs became themselves the victims of a colossal countercritical campaign. Known as the "antirightist campaign" and orchestrated in its details by the newly appointed secretary-general of the Communist Party, Deng Xiaoping, this harsh counteroffensive destroyed hundreds of thousands of lives, leading those found guilty to lose their Party posts and writers' jobs, and to be sent to remote rural areas or to "reform themselves through labor" in some form of detention center. In many cases they were not rehabilitated until the 1970s or later. The cost to China's scientific and economic establishment was as high as it was to the creative arts, literature, and education generally. It was often foreign-educated scholars with advanced intellectual skills who had been lulled into speaking out the loudest, and their attempt to truly make a hundred flowers bloom led to their being condemned as "poisonous weeds" for life.

Though infinitely more complex in its origins than the

Hundred Flowers Movement, and unfolding on a far greater scale across the whole of China, the Great Leap Forward ended in catastrophe and famine, a famine that between 1960 and 1961 cost at least 20 million lives. The Great Leap, in Mao's mind, would combine the imperatives of large-scale cooperative agriculture with a close-to-utopian vision of the ending of distinctions between occupations, sexes, ages, and levels of education. By compressing the hundreds of thousands of existing cooperatives—the number had passed 700,000 by late 1957—into around 20,000 giant communes, with all land owned by the state and worked in common, Mao believed that China as a whole would reap the immense benefits of scale and of flexibility. Communal kitchens and laundries would release women from chores to perform more constructive agricultural tasks; rural laborers would learn to build backyard steel furnaces and supplement China's iron and steel production in the urban factories; local militia would increase the combat effectiveness of the People's Liberation Army by allowing them to concentrate on high-priority military matters; communal schools would end the literacy gap; barefoot doctors would bring health care within the reach of every peasant; and collections of people's poems would swell the national cultural heritage. An organizational ladder, moving up from the individual and family to the work team, the team to the production brigade, and the brigade to the commune and thence to the county and provincial Party secretaries, would speed the flow of orders from the top to the bottom of society and bring the Party's message effortlessly to all.

It was in the summer of 1958, at the seaside resort of Beidaihe—where the Communist leaders held an annual summer retreat in the beachside homes built long ago by the foreign imperialists—that Mao's euphoria reached its pinnacle.

The occasion was an enlarged meeting of the Politburo, the inner core of China's leaders, and Mao's remarks were scattered in separate speeches spread out over two weeks. In these musings, Mao shared with his senior colleagues a hope for China's future that had little contact with current reality. Referring to the Great Leap as a continuation of the previous blooming and contending among the Hundred Flowers, Mao professed to see in it the promise of a China without hunger in which the Chinese themselves would no longer pay for food and the surplus would be given away free to the poorer people elsewhere in the world. An extra billion or so added to China's population would make no difference. Deep plowing, close planting, reforestation, and the economies of scale made possible by enthusiastic massed labor power would produce this surplus, in which a third of China's land would lie fallow every year. The sprouts of Communism were already present, said Mao. Hard work and discipline would bring better health to everyone, just as Mao had experienced it in the cave dwellings during the civil war, and physicians would have nothing left to do except research. Mental labor would fuse with manual labor, and education would be merged with production. Nobody would need to put on airs—clothes would be indistinguishable in cut and texture, and would be as free as food. Differentiated wage systems would vanish, as would any need for private housing. Morality would improve so much in the new society that no supervision would be required, and all would have the inspired and selfless spirit that had been such a force in the past revolution, when "people died without asking anything in return." The whole of China would be a lush and landscaped park so that no one would even need to travel anymore to see the sights.

Whatever the listeners thought, none of them raised voices

in protest, and the Great Leap, with all its wild visions, became the policy of the nation in late 1958 and well into 1959. The peasants and workers performed prodigies of labor, working with almost no respite in the fields. Mao suggested the peasants might take off two days in every month to avoid overwork; industrial workers should sleep at their work sites, next to their machines, to save time wasted in commuting. All this was possible, as Mao had said, because the Chinese "people are very disciplined; this has impressed me profoundly. During my visit to Tianjin, tens of thousands of people gathered around me, but at a single wave of my hand everybody dispersed." Now, almost at a single wave of his hand, they had come together again. The future seemed to be Mao's for the taking.

Bleak Harvest

BOTH THE HUNDRED FLOWERS movement and the launching of the Great Leap show Mao more and more divorced from any true reality check. His scientific speculations, philosophical musings, and economic projections—when unmediated and unpolished by his own private secretaries and the outlying teams of party ideologues—seem in the raw to be extremely simple, if not simpleminded. And he himself seemed to care less and less for the consequences that might spring from his own erratic utterances.

For the strange fact was that Mao had created a world in which things could hardly be otherwise. With the world outside China, Mao had virtually no contact. In his conversations with Stalin in December 1949 and January 1950 there had been some fairly sharp exchanges, and there is no doubt that the Soviet leader had the domestic power and global prestige in the Communist movement to say whatever he liked to Mao. But Stalin died in 1953, and Mao made only one more trip to the Soviet Union, in late 1957. That was a formal occasion, to celebrate the fortieth anniversary of the Bolshevik Revolution, and Mao's speeches gave nothing away about his true feelings. Mao was not close to Khrushchev, who had angered him by giving the Chinese no warning before his denunciations of Stalin; and though Mao was critical of Stalin, too, in several of his off-the-cuff talks to Chinese cadres, his relations with Khrushchev were never cordial, and the two countries drifted steadily apart until their cultural and political ties were totally severed in 1960.

Mao saw numerous other foreign leaders in Beijing, but the meetings were generally shrouded in protocol, and visitors were unlikely to point out his shortcomings. Mao had never been to any foreign country except the Soviet Union, and he never visited any other place outside China until he died. As he had said in his 1958 Beidaihe speech, "Why tour the four continents," when China itself contains so much? Many of Mao's senior Communist colleagues had lived and studied abroad for considerable periods, and spoke one or more foreign languages. Mao, by the late 1950s, seems to have given up on the study of Russian, though his surviving son, Anqing, and his eldest daughter, Li Min, because of the war years they spent in the Soviet Union, were as at home in Russian as in Chinese. Though he continued to struggle away at English lessons, Mao found them tiring and would use minor illnesses as an excuse to give up on his English reading. When he wanted to read Lenin—as he did with *What Is to Be Done*, at the time of the antirightist campaign—he specifically asked his secretary to get him a Chinese version, not one in Russian or English.

Personal observation of social conditions was also a natural way to gather information about China, and as a youth Mao had excelled at this, compiling careful notes on the minutest gradations of economic strata and drawing bold conclusions from closely watched moments of violence and self-assertion by the poor. In the first few years after 1949 he enjoyed wandering around in the Chinese countryside and revisiting his home province of Hunan. The informal letters people sent from Shaoshan and Xiangtan in the earlier 1950s showed they were not yet overawed by their famous native son, and on the various swims Mao made in the Xiang River of Hunan, or the Yangtze just to the north, he seems to have had time for relaxed talks with villagers and a chance to get at least a nodding acquaintance with their concerns. But from the late 1950s onward, Mao traveled in his specially equipped train, with personal attendants and bodyguards always present, which further increased his isolation from the outside world. In the spring of 1956, when villagers living on the Xiang River near Changsha came to Mao with their problems, he told them to speak to the Hunan Communist cadres. At the same time he wrote a poem in classical meter extolling the joys of floating free with the current.

In normal circumstances, a further source of information for Mao about the true situation might have been his current wife, Jiang Qing. She was twenty years younger than Mao, and with her Shandong upbringing and early adulthood acting in films and theater in Shanghai, in addition to her long years in Yan'an and forced marches under extreme danger during the civil war period, she was certainly not without varied experience. But whereas in the early 1950s Mao would often mention her well-being casually in letters to friends, implying a reasonable level of intimacy, by 1956 the couple were growing estranged, though both were still living in Zhongnanhai. That same year Jiang Qing went to the Soviet Union for treatment of cervical cancer; according to later reminiscences by her Soviet physician, she told him that she and Mao were no longer sleeping together.

It may have been this ending of his third long personal and

sexual relationship that turned Mao's thoughts back so incessantly to Yang Kaihui. In January 1958, a poem that Mao had written the previous year in memory of his former wife—dead now for almost twenty-eight years—was published in *People's Daily*. Mao wrote it in response to a poem his friend Li Shuyi sent him about the death of her husband in a battle with the Guomindang in 1932, and both poems, especially his, were to receive over the next few months an outpouring of effusive critical acclaim in Chinese literary magazines. Mao's is indeed a moving poem, especially the second stanza:

> Chang E in her loneliness
> Spreads her billowing sleeves,
> As through the vast emptiness of space
> She dances for these virtuous souls.
> Suddenly word comes that down on Earth,
> The Tiger has been subdued.
> And the tears that they shed
> Fall like a torrent of rain.

According to Chinese legend, familiar to Mao's readers, Chang E stole the elixir of immortality from her husband and fled to the moon with it. But once there, she had no one to share her gift of immortality with and found herself living in the most intense loneliness. After receiving the poem from Li Shuyi—in answer to which he penned his own—Mao asked her to visit Yang Kaihui's grave at her birthplace in Banchang, outside Changsha, on his behalf. (He could, of course, have gone himself, but there is no record that he did.)

Other family members probably could give little frank advice to their country's chairman. His companion from the Jinggangshan and Jiangxi Soviet days, He Zizhen, was living on her own in Shanghai, and had had a breakdown in 1954 (according to one source, after hearing a broadcast made by Mao over the radio). Mao offered to pay for her neurologist from his publishing royalties, but his revolutionary comrade Chen Yi, then Shanghai's mayor, said that he would pay out of city funds. Similarly, it would have been impossible for Mao's children to voice unease over the political direction he was taking, though they were in touch with him in Beijing. The one surviving child of Mao and He, their daughter, Li Min, lived with Mao in Zhongnanhai and was attending Beijing Teachers College—she had already graduated from the attached girls' secondary school. Li Na, Mao's daughter with Jiang Qing, was also living in Zhongnanhai and attending school. (She entered Beijing University as a history major in 1961 and graduated in 1965.) Anqing, the surviving son from the marriage to Yang Kaihui, was hospitalized much of the time, and had not yet married. (In 1962 he wed the half sister of his late brother's widow.) Mao's brothers, his sisters, and his parents were all long since dead.

A further source of information for Mao on current needs and politics might have been the press or the radio, but these were controlled and administered by the Communist Party, and all items included there had undergone careful prior scrutiny for their political correctness. Such battles as raged in the press were between competing factions outside the press arena, who sought maximum publicity for their own point of view. Being an editor was both a risky and a high-profile job, bringing handsome perks but the promise of a speedy fall if one gauged the political currents wrongly. One can see such pitfalls clearly in the relationship between Mao and Deng Tuo, who served as the editor of the official Communist Party newspaper, *People's Daily*, in the crucial early years of the People's Republic, from the fall of 1949 until February 1959.

Deng Tuo's education, background, and political experience would have made him an invaluable source of advice to Mao, had such a relationship been possible within the existing Party environment of the time. Deng Tuo was the son of a Qing official and received an intensive education in both classical Chinese scholarship—including art connoisseurship and calligraphy—and in the new Western subjects of study. Drawn to the radical currents of the day, he joined the Communist Party in 1930, while a student in Shanghai. When the Japanese routed the Chinese armies in late 1937, Deng Tuo made his way north to the Communist base area adjacent to Yan'an known as the Shanxi-Chahar-Hebei region. Once there, he showed immense courage and ability in running a series of clandestine Communist newspapers, and in keeping a secret radio station on the air. Fluent in English, Deng Tuo frequently served as interpreter and publicist for Western journalists, doctors, or liaison personnel of various kinds, and his charm, immense learning, and dedication to the revolution deeply impressed his own superiors in the Party. No one can have been surprised when Deng Tuo was named editor of *People's Daily* once the Communists came to power.

Deng obviously was uneasy over many of Mao's new policies, but as editor of the most authoritative public voice of the Party he could not control the content and ideological slant of what he published, nor could he express his worries openly. The only way he could express his views was to delay putting items in the newspaper, to juggle the placement of stories inside the paper, or to hint at hidden truths by the juxtapositions of items. Deng survived his early years as editor well, but the events of the Hundred Flowers and the Great Leap stretched his tact and evasiveness to the breaking point. The first colossal dilemma Deng faced as editor was how to handle criticism from senior Party members opposed to Mao on the agricultural and industrial policies of the "Little Leap." In the summer of 1956, Deng printed the slogan announced by no less a dignitary than the finance minister himself that China should "oppose impetuosity and adventurism." He followed this up with an editorial—drafted by him, revised by the director of the Communist Central Committee's propaganda department, and reviewed by the senior Politburo member, Liu Shaoqi, in person—in which he repeated the call to "oppose impetuosity" and added that "in our actual work we should carefully and on the basis of facts consider what can be done more and more fast, and what cannot be done more and more fast."

For polemic, the words seemed muted enough, but the whole thrust against Mao's thinking was clear. Mao's reaction illustrated his own growing jumpiness about any challenges to his own ideological authority: he scrawled across his own copy of the editorial the three characters *bu kan le*, meaning literally "not read," though an alternative translation would be something like "not to read," or "not worth reading." The attempt to propagate the Hundred Flowers Movement also brought Mao into conflict with Deng, as did the newspaper's dilatoriness in publishing any version of Mao's February 1957 speech on contradictions. Even when Mao stumped Tianjin and Shanghai in late March and early April of 1957 to push the Hundred Flowers Movement, the paper gave his speeches minimal coverage.

The result was a showdown between Mao and Deng Tuo on April 10, 1957. Recalled in detail by one of Deng's colleagues present at the scene, it showed how far Mao now was from being willing to entertain alternate interpretations of policy. Deng and his staff were summoned after lunch to see Mao in his residence inside Zhongnanhai. When the editors entered the room, they found Mao sprawled on his bed, wearing just a pajama jacket, with a towel draped around his waist. The bed was piled with books, and he chain-smoked as he talked. Mao at once launched into a long diatribe against the *People's Daily* editorial policy, accusing Deng of running a "factional paper," not a "Party paper." He continued: "In the past I said you people were pedants running the paper. Wrong, I should say you're dead men running the paper." Deng tried to explain the complex Party mechanisms that cleared material for publication in *People's Daily*, but Mao snapped back, "Why make a secret of Party policy? . . . If Party papers are passive, Party leadership also becomes passive. There is a ghost in this. Where is the ghost?"

Turning to the other junior editors, who sat in a nervous semicircle around the bed, Mao asked them why they had all been so silent: "If you want to raise criticism with Deng Tuo, the most he can do is fire you. How come not even a breeze got through, how come not one of you wrote a letter to the Party Center reporting the situation?" When Deng responded by offering his resignation, stating that he had acted sincerely and in good faith, Mao erupted with the bathroom language that he employed often in his speeches now, as if to emphasize his rough-and-ready rustic background: "I don't believe that sincerity and good faith of yours! You only know the comings and goings of limousines, you live in luxury. Now, shit or get off the pot."

In the long, almost-four-hour harangue that followed, Mao

accused the paper of hiding the achievements of the Chinese people by lowering the figures reported of their good harvests. Mao was determined to make the intellectuals serve the proletarians, he said, just as he had already cowed the national capitalists. Any use of Marxism to dismiss his own ideas he rejected as "dogmatism." He was going to resign the state chairmanship soon, said Mao (he actually did so in the spring of 1959), and he would then start writing his own regular column in the paper. When one of Mao's confidential secretaries, who had been present throughout, reminded the chairman that he had personally approved many of the policies and procedures he was now attacking, Mao responded, "Well, if it was like that, I was confused." Deng was dismissed as editor that June.

The intervention of the confidential secretary highlights another of the groups that might have brought Mao detailed knowledge of what was going on around the country. These secretaries were a high-caliber group, with proven revolutionary credentials. Some of them did funnel information to Mao when they felt he needed it, but they could go on inspection tours only when specifically instructed to do so. The same was true of Mao's elite guardsmen, many of them former peasants, who had a rough practicality and an absence of education that appealed to Mao. Many in Mao's entourage were simply overwhelmed by his formidable reputation and his famous rages— the doctor Li Zhisui, for example, who wrote a long and apparently frank appraisal of Mao after the chairman's death, makes it clear that he never risked alienating his master by raising unpleasant subjects. Thus the extraordinary and ultimately disastrous experiment of the Great Leap was continued across China.

What is most bizarre about these years is that one side of

Mao was deeply skeptical about the path onto which he had guided the country. When people he liked and trusted asked him to spare them the rigors of laboring in the countryside on Great Leap projects, he was willing to write letters in their behalf to have them excused. He did just that for the nanny who had looked after his three sons with Yang Kaihui back in the 1930s, when local cadres ordered her to report for a work assignment at the end of 1957. Yet his other side would not tolerate direct criticism of the Great Leap at any level. This profound and disastrous ambiguity was matched by his own senior colleagues, all veterans of the revolution and deeply experienced in social organization and economic planning, who had been nervous about the ventures of both the Hundred Flowers and the Great Leap, but in their eagerness to promote the country's growth and to shelter their own careers, never took decisive action to check the headlong course of events.

This can be seen in a transcript of Party meetings held in Wuchang, on the Yangtze, in November 1958. Here, in a self-contradictory maze of comments and responses, Mao showed he was fully aware of the incredible levels of violence in the mass campaigns, the dangers of famine sweeping the country, the need to send investigative teams out to check the reality of production, the impossibility of reaching the steel, grain, and earth-removal quotas, the falsified reporting at all levels that was riddling the entire venture with contradictions, and the faked compliance with which millions of peasants greeted the Party center's impossible demands. As Mao told his assembled cadres, poetry was not the same as economic reality, and this was not a "dream" from which one would simply "wake up." And yet when in the summer of 1959 the distinguished marshal of the Red Army and minister of defense Peng Dehuai made similar points at the Lushan meeting of the Central Committee, which had convened to discuss all aspects of the Great Leap, Mao exploded with rage.

At the conference, Peng presented his critical views in a circumspect way, not by grandstanding but by submitting a personal letter to the chairman. In that letter, written during the night of July 12 and hand-delivered to Mao on the thirteenth, Peng pointed out that despite many increases in production during the Great Leap so far, it had been a story of both "losses and gains" (he reversed the normal phrase "gains and losses"). Exaggeration had run through the whole campaign, and in steel production especially there had been a host of mistakes. Slogans and projections had been faulty, and there were clearly many "leftist" mistakes—mistakes one could also describe as "petty-bourgeois fanaticism."

Peng had intended his letter to be private, but Mao determined to strike back. Mao's entire reputation was at stake, for Peng was known to have traveled earlier in 1959 through many areas of China, checking things out for himself, including Mao's own home village of Shaoshan. Mao had just fulsomely praised the Great Leap in Shaoshan in a poem that linked the heroic Hunan peasant uprisings of 1927 to what he saw as the equally heroic reality of the present:

Cursed by the flow of memories,
I am back in my native place thirty-two years ago.
Red flags flutter from the spears of the enslaved peasants,
As the landlords raise their whips in cruel hands.
It took many sacrifices to make us so strong
That we dared tell sun and moon to bring a new day.
In delight I watch the waving rows of rice and beans,
While all around the heroes return through the evening
    haze.

By contrast, Peng, having been in the same village at almost the same time, had likened the Great Leap experiments in Hunan to "beating a gong with a cucumber." And, though he had not put this in his letter, during one of the opening small group discussions at Lushan, Peng had reported on his own visit to Shaoshan (now converted into a commune), saying that though indeed production there had risen by 14 percent, this increase was achieved "with much assistance and large loans from the state. The Chairman has also visited this commune. I asked the Chairman what was his finding. He said that he had not talked about the matter. In my opinion, he had."

Mao's response was tactically bold and totally successful. He ordered his staff to make multiple copies of Peng's letter, and had it distributed to the 150 senior cadres present. Then in a series of face-to-face meetings, he challenged them either to accept his version of events or to side publicly with Peng. If they did side with Peng, said Mao, he would raise another army, a truly *red* one this time, and would start the guerrilla wars in the hills all over again. Confronted by this stark choice, not a single cadre sided publicly with Peng, even though it is possible that some of them—in prior conversation—might actually have primed Peng to write some of the things that he had. At the close of the Lushan meetings, Mao dismissed Peng from all his posts and relegated him to political limbo.

The result of the Lushan plenum was thus not only that Peng's warnings were totally rejected but that the principles of the Great Leap were reaffirmed by Mao and by all his senior colleagues. They did this despite the knowledge that all the previous figures for production had indeed been gross exaggerations, pointing to totally unrealizable levels of achievement. By branding anyone who criticized the concept of the Leap as being a "right opportunist" (by implication in league with Peng Dehuai), Mao made it impossible for any of his Party colleagues—junior or senior—to publicly call the Leap into question. Mao himself ringingly endorsed the huge public dining halls: "The moral is that one must not capitulate in the face of difficulties. Things like people's communes and collective mess halls have deep economic roots. They should not nor can they be blown away by a gust of wind." The need for active support of the Leap ideology was given a new twist in an editorial in the now totally obedient *People's Daily* of August 1959. The paper argued that a failure to identify and criticize the "rightists" would be tantamount to willing the failure of the Leap. By the end of the month, the paper editorialized that "the hostile forces within the country and abroad" and the "right opportunists within the party" had clearly failed to derail the Leap: "The people's communes have not collapsed. We have therefore the right to say that the people's communes will never collapse."

Thus it was that, as Mao yielded up the position of head of state to his fellow Hunanese Liu Shaoqi, giving up much wearisome protocol that he had never much relished, and "retired to the second line" as he put it, to devote more time to theoretical work, the Leap was pushed to new heights. In the face of mounting evidence of poor harvests, and with China being hit by colossal floods—some of them the worst in a century—crops almost ready for harvest were uprooted in favor of new planting plans, deep plowing to a level of three meters or more was pushed at Mao's behest, and hundreds of millions of peasants, many exhausted by a year of ceaseless projects, were pushed into the same pattern of totally unrealistic expectations. By 1960 famine began to strike large areas of the country. Peng Dehuai was kept out of sight, his criticism ignored. For two years the crisis deepened as the Party continued to enforce the laws on grain procurement from fields where almost no crops grew. The Maoist vision had finally tumbled into nightmare.

Fanning the Flames

IN 1960 THE FAMINE tightened its grip across the country, exacerbated not only by a devastating drought that ruined crops on almost half of China's farmland, but also by an erratic pattern of south-to-north typhoons that brought violent wind damage and murderous flash floods. In many areas for which accurate figures became available, between a fifth to a half of all the villagers died, with Anhui province perhaps suffering the most. And yet, so pervasive was the force of Mao's words at Lushan, that many of the fundamental principles of the Great Leap were maintained. Communes continued to be run on the radical and egalitarian principles enunciated in 1957 and 1958. Extraction of rural "surpluses" continued, to support industry and subsidize food prices in the cities. Many peasants were taken from the land to boost the industrial labor force in the cities, where urban communes were now introduced widely, to bring the same principles of mixed and intensified production to factories, schools, and offices.

Especially during 1960, however, the focus of the leaders' attention was not on the exact details of the domestic crisis. Instead, they were compelled to focus on the Soviet Union, which had mocked the extravagant claims put forward in the Great Leap and continued with its own policies of de-Stalinization. In particular, the leaders had to work out how to find the funds and personnel to continue the various projects abandoned by the Soviet advisers when they were pulled out of China that year. These included China's atomic-bomb program, and also the oil fields in China's northeast. Mao's own writings were focused on polemics against Khrushchev and on attempts to express his interpretation of China's place in the pattern of world revolution. Only rarely did he comment specifically on Chinese economic matters.

In 1961 this began to change. Early in the year, Mao acceded to his colleagues' arguments that the Leap be rolled back, that productive laborers be returned to their communes, and that peasants be allowed to raise some food and livestock again on small private plots near their homes. Most aspects of communal living were canceled. Though Mao rejected Khrushchev's unexpected offer of Soviet grain shipments to reduce the stress of hunger, the Central Committee planners decided to buy large quantities of grain from Canada. And in late January, Mao summoned one of his confidential political secretaries, Tian Jiaying, who had worked with him since 1948, to organize and dispatch three teams—each consisting of seven men—to undertake an intensive investigation of the exact situation in sample communes in three different provinces: Guangdong, Hunan, and Zhejiang. Apparently recalling his previous experiences with rural investigations in the early days of the revolution, Mao had returned to the realization that there was no substitute for hard facts in trying to come to grips with harsh reality.

We do not know whether Mao specifically turned over in his mind the contrast between his languid days in Shaoshan during the summer of 1959—chatting to elderly peasants over a banquet, lolling in the warm, shallow waters of the new mass-labor-generated Shaoshan reservoir, and poetically praising the peasants' triumphs—with Peng Dehuai's hard-hitting questions and bleak statistics on the same area. But clearly Mao was now trying to find out what had gone wrong. The team sent to Guangdong province was to be led by Chen Boda, his trusted aide since the two men's dialectical-materialism discussions of 1937; the Hunan team was led by Hu Qiaomu, another close political aide and secretary to Mao (he had been present at the meeting where Deng Tuo was called "a dead man"). Others in the groups included members of Liu Shaoqi's staff, propaganda specialists, economists, and statisticians.

Each group of seven was instructed to focus on two production brigades: one well-off, one poor. Secretary Tian pooled their conclusions and summarized them for Mao. His summary was bold and unambiguous: private plots should be allowed and compensation paid for wrongly confiscated property, the scale of the communes should be cut back, peasants should follow their own views on communal living or cooking, and cadre corruption should be addressed directly. This time Mao appeared to see that a reversal of policy was essential. He drafted—again with Tian—a document in sixty sections that addressed the main perceived problems in the communes. After Mao—who now felt he had the facts at his command—had taunted other leaders for their ignorance of the real situation in the countryside, they, too, began to undertake their own intensive explorations and were indeed horrified by what they found. Liu Shaoqi and his wife carried out their investigation in person, not through surrogates, focusing on Hunan for over a month (they also visited Mao's old home village of Shaoshan). Everywhere they found a pattern of evasion, a reluctance to speak out, for fear of the consequences, and serious abuses of authority by the brigade officials, even those who were from poor peasant backgrounds themselves. Over the following year, Liu and his senior colleagues slowly moved China back to a more rational level of planned allocations in agriculture and industry, which would make the household or "team" the basic economic unit of accounting, though the commune system survived, with communes subdivided into smaller units.

During this entire period, Mao was smarting under an additional series of slights: a calculated move by many in the Party to downplay the role of the "Thought of Mao" in the fabric of the People's Republic. It was at the 1945 congress that the Constitution of the Communist Party had been altered to include Mao's thought as its guiding principle. Mao had acquiesced in dropping the phrase from a revision of the Constitution that was promulgated in 1956, which made sense in light of the denunciations of Stalin in the Soviet Union and a general nervousness about the "cult of personality." But Mao had not intended his acceptance of that formal change to herald a change in the general status of his writings. But that is just what began to occur after the Lushan meetings, as statements were issued by the Communist Youth League that the phrase "Thought of Mao," though sometimes essential, should not be overused. Fewer copies of Mao's works were now available; a shortage of paper due to the Great Leap and the pressing needs for printing more school textbooks were both cited by Mao's colleagues as the reasons. A report of the Party Center's propaganda department in March 1960 warned against "vulgarization" of Mao's works by attributing various triumphs to their beneficent effect—breakthroughs in medicine, for example, or triumphs in table tennis competitions. Liu Shaoqi, now head of state, instructed that the phrase "Thought of Mao" not be used in propaganda directed at foreign audiences. Other senior Party leaders commented publicly that Mao's thought could in no way be said to surpass Marxism-Leninism, indeed that after the definitive analyses of political economy and imperialism by Marx and Lenin there was really no need for further discussion of those topics.

Two key Party figures, however, decided to risk their colleagues' irritation by publicly reaffirming their faith in Mao's thought; they were Mao's public security chief, Kang Sheng, and the army general Lin Biao, whom Mao had appointed as minister of defense to replace the disgraced Peng Dehuai. Lin Biao was especially fulsome in talking with his own military officers, continuing to refer to Mao's thought as the "pinnacle of Marxism-Leninism in the present era." And in an enthusiastic accolade when the volume of Mao's *Selected Works* which included the period of World War II and the civil war was published late in 1961, Lin Biao wrote that the victory in that war was also the victory of Mao's thought; for the army as a whole "our present important fighting task [is] to arm our minds with Mao Zedong's Thought, to defend the purity of Marxism-Leninism, and combat every form of ideological trend of modern revisionism."

The ground was being laid for a new kind of division within the Party, one that pitted those who were truly "red"—the believers in Mao's thought and the purifying power of trusting the masses—against those who based their prestige and policies on their specific expertise, whether that lay in precise economic planning, advanced education, or mastery of bureaucratic procedures. Between 1962 and 1966 this struggle was fought out, sometimes in public and sometimes silently, as Mao worked to prepare for the kind of renewed assault from the moral guerrilla high ground of which he had spoken in his attack at Lushan on Peng Dehuai.

To double-check his sense of how the peasants were reacting to the changes in rural policy, Mao turned again to his trusted secretary Tian Jiaying. This time Tian was to concentrate his work on three places in Hunan: Mao's own village of Shaoshan, Mao's grandparents' village, and Liu Shaoqi's home village, which was not far away from the other two. In a farewell party for Tian and his colleagues, held at a guest house in Wuchang, Mao urged them not to boss people around but to listen carefully and carry no preconceptions with them—except their belief in Marxism and knowledge of the historical context of what they saw. To his surprise, Tian found that while the peasants in Liu's home village were comparatively content with the improvement to their current situation brought by the return of private plots and the shrinkage in the units of organization, those in Mao's village were in favor of two policies that would be far to the "right" of the current line: these were either to apportion out production on the basis of each household (rather than any larger unit whatsoever), or else to go back to the pre-cooperative phase altogether and to divide the fields once again among the households. Nervous about the findings, Tian left Shaoshan for Shanghai, where Mao was currently living in another guest house. Though Tian sent his report in advance, Mao had clearly not read it. Instead he listened to Tian's oral report in silence, and then made a revealing comment: "We want to follow the mass line, but there are times when we cannot completely heed the masses. For example, if they want to distribute production on the basis of the household, we cannot listen to them." Tian also got phone calls from the head of the Central Committee's organization department in Beijing, who was eager to discuss his findings, and met with Deng Xiaoping and Liu Shaoqi. He found that virtually all the leaders except for Mao favored some kind of redistribution of production based on the household.

It was clear that there was now little meeting of the minds between Mao and his own senior colleagues, apart from the small group of those boosting his thoughts. As Mao got older, he had apparently further increased his isolation from his own people, even as he claimed to speak in their name. The Mao who had so often praised the virtues of living in caves, now stayed at a series of luxurious guest houses—provided for him by Party officials—in different parts of China. It was people like Tian who now acted as his eyes and ears.

In addition, it seems clear that Mao's lifestyle had not endeared him to his revolutionary colleagues. At the now more frequent dances in Zhongnanhai, in his private room aboard his own personal railway train, and in the numerous guest houses he visited, Mao entertained a succession of young women. News of these liaisons helped spread an aura of moral vulnerability around the chairman, which was confirmed when his private railroad car was bugged by overly zealous security officials. They were not discreet about what they learned, enraging Mao when he heard what they had done. Mao's entourage of guards were also, at least in some cases, exploitative of their power, often corrupt, and involved in sexual liaisons of their own.

Somewhat paradoxically, it was at this very time that Mao's own family began to settle down, apparently constructively, into the society around them. His only surviving son, Anqing, whom as recently as 1956 Mao was still describing to friends as "crippled with illness," was married at last in 1962 at the age of thirty-nine. Anqing's wife was the half sister of his elder brother

Anying's widow. Fluent in Russian, like Anqing himself, she entered Beijing University's department of Chinese the same year, and graduated in 1966. Urged on by Mao, Anying's widow remarried around the same time. Li Min, He Zizhen's surviving daughter, graduated from teachers college and married a graduate of the air force academy. She subsequently worked in the military defense bureau, while her husband taught in the academy. Jiang Qing's daughter, Li Na, entered Beijing University's history department in 1961 and graduated in 1965. She was to be a key link between Mao and the student community in 1966.

Mao seems to have encouraged his immediate family to lead as ordinary a life as possible and not to take an active part in politics, but he was not so protective of his brothers' families. Mao Yuanxin, for example, the son of Mao's younger brother Mao Zemin (executed in Xinjiang in 1943) was enrolled in the Harbin Institute of Military Engineering in 1964, and Mao used him as a foil for many of his own ideas. Their exchanges were later published. From Mao's questions to his nephew, we can see that he was feeling out a field for himself, in which the next round of the battle could be fought to his advantage. The fact that there was a definite enemy—the forces of "bourgeois revisionism" inside China determined to undermine the revolution—was already firming up in Mao's mind. These enemies might be found anywhere: in rural production brigades and urban factories, in Party committees and public security departments, and in the ministry of culture and the film industry. They were even among the students in Mao Yuanxin's own institute, listening secretly to overseas radio broadcasts and filling their diaries with subversive material. "They" were also behind the rote system of lecturing and the pointless examinations that schools used to judge a person's performance.

Now, at the age of seventy, Mao was clearly obsessed with revolutionary continuity and his belief that the young people like Yuanxin would have to bear the standard forward. Five elements were essential in this succession, Mao told his nephew: one must be a genuine Marxist-Leninist; one must be willing to serve the masses wholeheartedly; one must work with the majority and accept their criticisms, even if the criticisms seemed misplaced at the time; one must be a model of obedient discipline under the strictures of democratic centralism; and one must be modest about oneself, always ready to indulge in self-criticism. Looking at his nephew, Mao added the harsh judgment: "You grew up eating honey, and thus far you have never known suffering. In future, if you do not become a rightist, but rather a centrist, I shall be satisfied. You have never suffered, how can you be a leftist?"

With these last words, Mao had posed a question that was to obsess him and many of China's youth into the early years of the Cultural Revolution. His answer was to be based on the idea that waning leftist revolutionary activism could be regenerated by identifying the enemies correctly, and then using all one's ingenuity in rooting them out and destroying them. Mao had stated in the past that it was necessary to "set fires" every few years to keep the revolution alive. But doing that could also frighten people: "It's certainly not easy to set a fire to burn oneself. I've heard that around this area there were some people who had second thoughts and didn't set a big fire." Mao came to see his mission as partly to set the fire, but also to teach the young to do it for themselves.

In this strangely apocalyptic mission, Mao found a loose association of allies. One was the defense minister, Lin Biao, who was willing to lead the People's Liberation Army forward into revolution, via the "little red book" of Mao's thought, which

Lin commissioned in 1964 and ordered every soldier to read. A year later Lin Biao ordered the abolition of insignia, Soviet-style uniforms, and other signs of officer status throughout the army, re-creating—at least in Mao's mind—an image of the simpler guerrilla aura of military life with which Mao had so long been associated. A second group of allies consisted of certain intellectuals and cadres, many of them based in Shanghai, who had a strongly leftist orientation and were genuinely dismayed by what they saw as the backward-looking direction of industrial and rural policy. A third was centered on Mao's wife, Jiang Qing, who for twenty years after their marriage in Yan'an had not been active in politics. But in 1956, after returning from her medical trip to the Soviet Union, she began to take a lively interest in the current state of film and theater in China. Gradually she formed a nucleus of fellow believers who sought to reinstill revolutionary attitudes into the cultural world and to root out those revisionist elements that—she agreed with Mao—were lurking everywhere. A fourth ally was Kang Sheng, a revolutionary Shanghai labor organizer and spymaster in the 1920s, later trained in police techniques in the Soviet Union. He had introduced Mao to Jiang Qing in Yan'an, and later became head of the Central Committee's security apparatus and of the Central Party School. Kang Sheng had been a pioneer in orchestrating a literary inquisition to prove that rightists were "using novels to promote anti-Party activities."

It was natural for these disparate forces to gradually coalesce, to find novelists, dramatists, historians, and philosophers on whom to pile their criticisms, and to use Shanghai as a base for mass campaigns that could also be coordinated with the army's various cultural departments. Once the apparatus of leftist criticism was in place in the cultural sphere, it could easily be switched to tackle problems of education in schools and universities, the municipal Party committees that were technically in charge of those cultural realms or educational systems, and the individual Party leaders to whom those committees reported. If galvanized from the center, a remarkable force might be generated.

By late 1965 this was exactly what began to happen. Mao was frustrated with the laggardly implementation of revolutionary policies, and genuinely suspicious of his own bureaucracy. He had grown to distrust the head of state, Liu Shaoqi, and to be skeptical about Liu's ability to guide the revolution after Mao. Mao also had grown more hostile to intellectuals as the years went by—perhaps because he knew he would never really be one, not even at the level of his own secretaries, whom he would commission to go to the libraries to track down classical sources for him and help with historical references. Mao knew, too, that scholars of the old school like Deng Tuo, the man he had summarily ousted from the *People's Daily*, had their own erudite circles of friends with whom the pursued leisurely hours of classical connoisseurship, which was scarcely different from the lives they might have enjoyed under the old society. They wrote elegant and amusing essays, which were printed in various literary newspapers, that used allegory and analogy to tease the kind of "commandism" that had been so present in the Great Leap, and indeed in the Communist leadership as a whole. It was surely of such men that Mao was thinking when he wrote: "All wisdom comes from the masses. I've always said that intellectuals are the most lacking in intellect. The intellectuals cock their tails in the air, and they think, 'If I don't rank number one in all the world, then I'm at least number two.'"

Mao did not precisely orchestrate the coming of the Cultural Revolution, but he established an environment that made it possible and helped to set many of the people and issues in place. In November 1965 a new round of polemics appeared in a Shanghai journal, attacking the historian Wu Han, who was the direct subordinate of the powerful Party boss Peng Zhen, controller of a five-man group that was the arbiter of the Beijing cultural realm. Peng Zhen was unprepared to handle the onslaught, though publication of the article in Beijing was blocked by his staff. Seizing on the chance disruption as a good trigger for action, Mao moved swiftly to remove the head of the Central Committee's general office, which controlled the flow of crucial information for senior Party leaders. It must have been an added inducement to Mao that this man was Yang Shangkun, who had ordered the bugging devices planted in Mao's personal train and in the guest houses where he stayed. In Yang's place, Mao appointed the head of the central Beijing garrison, whom he knew to be fiercely loyal.

At the same time, Lin Biao began to replace key personnel at the top of the military, including the current army chief of staff and former minister of security Luo Ruiqing. In March 1966, after months of relentless questioning about his political loyalties and his attitudes toward political indoctrination in the army ranks, as well as a major series of "struggle sessions" with his inquisitors, Luo tried to commit suicide by jumping from a building. Mao's wife, Jiang Qing, joined the fray by briefing army commanders on the bourgeois decadence and corruption in the arts, which led to the publication of a joint "army forum on literature and art work." Mao had already, in a meeting with his secretaries, shared with them his conviction that the works of the historian Wu Han were intended to be defenses of Peng Dehuai in his earlier struggle at Lushan, and he proceeded to deepen the attacks on the Beijing party and cultural establishment. Lin Biao sharpened the tension by warning that the "right" was planning a coup against Mao. Security was tightened in the Zhongnanhai residential area. Two men knew, as well as any in China, what all this must portend. They were Deng Tuo, the former editor of *People's Daily*, and Tian Jiaying, Mao's confidential secretary for eighteen years, who had reported negatively on the peasants' feelings about communes. In the last weeks of May, both men committed suicide.

Much of this struggle had taken place in secret, or at least in the well-insulated world of the Party hierarchy. But in late May, some Beijing University teachers put up wall posters denouncing the rightists, or "capitalist-roaders," in their campuses and in the cultural bureaucracy; Mao endorsed the posters, and students began to follow suit, with attacks against their own teachers. *People's Daily* editorialized in favor of the dissidents, and the movement spread to other cities in China, and from colleges to high schools. Groups of students began to wear paramilitary uniforms with red armbands and to declare themselves Red Guards and defenders of Chairman Mao. Mao himself, who had been watching these events from the security of a guest house in the celebrated beauty spot of Hangzhou, traveled in July to Wuhan and took a leisurely swim down the Yangtze, which was rapturously publicized across the nation as proof of the chairman's energy and fitness.

Returning to Beijing, Mao reconstituted the Politburo Standing Committee, to remove or demote those he had identified as his enemies. As for himself, Mao wrote in a brief editorial comment that appeared in *People's Daily*: "My wish is to join all the comrades of our party to learn from the masses, to continue to be a schoolboy." In August, with the oracular pronouncement that "to rebel is justified," and that it was good "to bombard the headquarters," Mao donned military uniform and from the top of Tiananmen reviewed hundreds of thousands of chanting students, accepting from them a Red Guard armband as evidence of his support. By September, several of the rallies were attended by a million people, who began to flock to Beijing from around China. The students from Beijing, in turn, began to travel the countryside in squads—free train travel was made available to them—to spread the word of what was now called the Cultural Revolution.

The violence of the Cultural Revolution was manifested at two levels. One of these was orchestrated from the political center, which was now controlled by a small group totally loyal to Mao, through what was called "The Central Case Examination Group," chaired by China's premier Zhou Enlai but directly accountable to Mao. In its heyday this group was composed of eleven Party members, including Jiang Qing, Chen Boda, and Kang Sheng. Under this leadership group were three bureaus that were assigned their own cases and worked closely with the Beijing garrison command, the army general staff, and the Ministry of Public Security. They investigated 1,262 "principal cases" and an unknown number of "related case offenders."

The job of the three bureaus was to prove the correctness of "rightist" charges—including being Taiwan or Guomindang spies, or "Khrushchev-type persons"—and to use whatever means were necessary to achieve that goal. Torture, sleep deprivation, round-the-clock group interrogations, withholding of food, and many types of mental and physical pressure were used by the case investigators—in virtually all cases their victims were prominent or even once-revered revolutionaries. Peng Dehuai was brought back from Sichuan to face his own group of investigators. Incarcerated in high-security prisons (of which Qincheng was the most terrifyingly notorious), the victims could not write letters home or see family. Letters they wrote to Mao or Zhou Enlai requesting more compassionate treatment were filed away, unread. Only "confessions" were considered a tolerable form of writing.

These political prisoners only encountered the outside "revolutionary masses" at carefully orchestrated occasions. Red Guard groups would use printed forms to apply to "borrow" one of the victims, as long as they were "returned promptly." Red Guard units might have to pay the cost of renting a place for these confrontations, which would then be advertised in advance. Certain "struggle rallies" were postponed in case of rain, and some victims were in such demand that their appearances had to be limited to three denunciations a week. Liu Shaoqi died from these experiences, as did Peng Dehuai. Deng Xiaoping survived, perhaps because Mao only intended to intimidate him, not to destroy him altogether. This system of case investigation was spread systematically to the provinces, and by the end of the Cultural Revolution in 1976 as many as two million cadres had been investigated by these or similar means.

The second level of cultural revolutionary violence was unorchestrated, coursing down its own channels in an only vaguely designated direction, in search of rightists or "feudal remnants," "snakes and monsters," or "people in authority taking the capitalist road." An announcement from the "Beijing Number 26 Middle School Red Guards," dated August 1966, gave the kind of program that was to be followed by countless others. Every street was to have a quotation from Chairman Mao prominently displayed, and loudspeakers at every intersection and in all parks were to broadcast his thought. Every household as well as all trains and buses, bicycles and pedicabs, had to have a picture of Mao on its walls. Ticket takers on trains and buses should all declaim Mao's thought. Every bookstore had to stock Mao's quotations, and every hand in China had to hold one. No one could wear blue jeans, tight pants, "weird women's outfits," or have "slick hairdos or wear rocket shoes." No perfumes or beauty creams could be used. No one could keep pet fish, cats, or dogs, or raise fighting crickets. No shop could sell classical books. All those identified by the masses as landlords, hooligans, rightists, and capitalists had to wear a plaque identifying themselves as such whenever they went out. The minimum amount of persons living in any room could be three—all other space had to be given to the state housing bureaus. Children should criticize their elders, and students their teachers. No one under thirty-five might smoke or drink. Hospital service would be simplified, and "complicated treatment must be abolished"; doctors had to write their prescriptions legibly, and not use English words. All schools and colleges were to combine study with productive labor and farmwork. As a proof of its own transformation, the "Number 26 Middle School" would change its name, effectively immediately, to "The Maoism School."

The number of victims from the uncoordinated violence of the Cultural Revolution is incalculable, but there were many millions. Some of these were killed, some committed suicide. Some were crippled or scarred emotionally for life. Others were tormented for varying periods of time, for an imprecise number of "crimes," such as having known foreigners, owned foreign books or art objects, indulged in classical studies, been dictatorial teachers, or denigrated Mao or the Party through some chance remark. Children suffered for their parents' or grandparents' deeds, or sought to clear themselves of such charges by exhibiting unusual "revolutionary zeal," which might include trashing their own parents' apartments, beating up their school-teachers, or going to border areas to "serve the people" and "learn from the masses." Many families destroyed their own art objects, burned or shredded their family photographs, diaries, and letters, all of which might be purloined by roving Red Guards. Many Red Guards units fought each other, sometimes to the death, divided along lines of local allegiance or class background, or by occupation, as in the case of some labor union members, construction workers, even prison wardens.

The tiny figure atop the rostrum at Tiananmen, waving his hand in a slow sideways motion to the chanting sea of red flags and little red books spread out before him as far as the eye could see, had only the faintest inklings of the emotions passing through the minds of the weeping faithful. It was enough that they were there, chanting and with tears in their eyes. It was enough that to them he had become, at last, the "Great Helmsman, great teacher, great leader, and the Red, Red sun in their hearts."

Embers

AT A WORK CONFERENCE with the Party leaders in late August 1966, Mao told his colleagues that matters seemed to be developing satisfactorily: "In my opinion, we should let the chaos go on for a few months and just firmly believe that the majority is good and only the minority bad." The best thing would be to wait four months and see what happened. Let the students take to the streets, let them write "big character posters." And "let the foreigners take pictures" of all this if they wanted to. It was of no importance what the imperialists thought.

Yet before the four months were up, Mao felt a touch of apprehension. At a follow-up meeting of the Central Work Conference on October 25, 1966, Mao reminded his colleagues that he was formally only "in the second line," and hence did "not take charge of day-to-day work" anymore. He had taken this second place deliberately, to build up their prestige, so that "when I go to see God there won't be such a big upheaval in the State." The result of this policy, however, had been that "there are some things I should have kept a grip on which I did not. So I am responsible; we cannot just blame them." With this elliptical apology over, Mao admitted that he had been swept away by the pace of events, like everyone else. "The time was so short and the events so violent" that the Red Guards had erupted and taken things into their own hands. "Since it was I who caused the havoc, it is understandable if you have some bitter words for me."

Yet, as he had done in 1959, after being criticized by Peng Dehuai, Mao continued to pursue the policies that he knew might not be working in the short term, but from which he still expected great things. The early stage of the revolution lasted twenty-eight years, he reminded his listeners, from 1921 to 1949. It was now only five months since the first moments of the Cultural Revolution—"perhaps the movement may last another five months, or even longer." In the earlier stage of the revolution, "our path gradually emerged in the course of practice." The same would be true again, for "things can change, things can improve." They would all have to work together, to benefit from the new world of change into which events had plunged them.

Students, however, were one thing, and workers and People's Liberation Army troops were another. In the course of those next few months, through which Mao had said they must watch things develop, two issues surfaced that had to be addressed. One was whether the industrial workers should be allowed to exploit the situation by uniting (or even striking) to achieve higher pay, more autonomy, and better working conditions. With few exceptions, the opinion of even the radical Cultural Revolutionary leaders was that they should not be allowed to do so, and steps were taken to curb the power of those workers' groups that had begun to emerge. The second issue was what the role of the army should be, now that under Lin Biao's enthusiastically pro-Maoist rhetorical guidance many Red Guard units were bringing economic and political chaos all across the country. Again, the ultimate decision was a conservative one (though it was given a leftist-sounding air): the political leadership vacuum that had now formed in many areas should not be filled by student or other Red Guard groups alone. In every workplace and community new "revolutionary committees" should be formed, each of which would be a "three way alliance" with three constituent parts: the People's Liberation Army; experienced party cadres who had been screened and cleared of any charge of being counterrevolutionaries or "capitalist-roaders"; and representatives of the radical mass organizations who had been recently "steeled" in revolutionary experience.

Mao himself never wrote a single, comprehensive analysis of what he intended to achieve by the Cultural Revolution, or of how he expected it to proceed. It does seem to have been a case of allowing theory to grow out of practice, as he had always interpreted the revolutionary process to be. Indeed he issued very few statements at all after the fall of 1966, and he did not speak to the masses in any public forums, with the lone exception of a few words he uttered over a microphone fitted to the rostrum on Tiananmen at the seventh mass Red Guards rally in November. The speech in its entirety ran as follows: "Long live comrades! You must let politics take command, go to the masses, and be with the masses. You must conduct the great proletarian Cultural Revolution even better." Even in the inner circles of Party leaders, where some of his words were transcribed and later circulated, his words and thoughts were far more condensed than they had been earlier. To the new leaders who had emerged from the literary wars of the Shanghai left, he reiterated the theme that in the Cultural Revolution one class was "toppling another," which constituted "a great revolution." He added that "many newspapers ought to be suspended," acknowledging in the same breath that "there must be newspapers." The key point, therefore, was who should run them, for "to revolt, one must first of all create a public opinion." Mao illuminated this thought with a personal flashback to the early 1920s, when he was running his journals in Hunan and also working on the early strikes of the printers: "We had no money, no publishing houses, no bicycles. When we edited newspapers, we got on intimate terms with printing workers. We chatted with them and edited articles at the same time." Mao had always loved the idea that political power could be strengthened through such informal and unstructured means.

Even these truncated ruminations were exceptions, however. From early 1967 onward, Mao let his thoughts be known mainly in the form of aphorisms or comments, just a few characters in length. These were printed as boxed editorials in *People's Daily*, usually on the front page. Thus after only a few seconds of reading, people all around the country could gauge their chairman's current thoughts. And probably these *were* his thoughts—there was no need to submit such brief and simple comments to Party scrutiny and to watch for possible deviations from the correct line. Mao *was* the line. As he observed in April 1968: "Except in the deserts, at every place of human habitation there is the left, the center, and the right. This will continue to be so 10,000 years hence."

Mao's own staff and family were not exempted from this process of struggle and violence, even though Red Guard units were not allowed into Zhongnanhai itself, or into the top-secret military installations such as those where scientists were working to develop the H-bomb (they had successfully constructed and detonated their own atomic bomb in October 1964, despite the refusal of the Soviets to help them). Indeed, Mao's nephew Mao Yuanxin tried to lead a group of Red Guards into just such a location, in Manchuria, but was prevented by the army force on duty. Having decided to ally himself with Jiang Qing, Yuanxin had become an important figure in the Cultural Revolution by this time, and Jiang Qing engineered his promotion to be a political commander in the Shenyang (Mukden) region. He even set up his own office inside Zhongnanhai. Mao's surviving son, Mao Anqing, seems to have been left alone, and his wife, Shaohua, joined the People's Liberation Army in 1966, on graduation from Beijing University, providing liaison between the family and the two key institutions in the Cultural Revolution. (They had a son, Xinyu, in 1971, Mao's second grandson.) Mao's eldest daughter, Li Min, was working in the Military Defense Bureau and came under harsh criticism for at least five months. Mao refused to help her in any way (he had refused to use his influence to help Jiang Qing also, when she came under criticism in the Yan'an rectification campaign), and Li Min and her husband had a difficult time. They had two children, a boy and a girl; the girl spent at least some of this bleak period living with her grandmother He Zizhen in Shanghai.

Mao's younger daughter, Li Na, graduated from Beijing University in 1965, and she kept her father abreast of student and faculty sentiment there in the early stages of the Cultural Revolution. She was working then as an editor of the People's Liberation Army newspaper, while living in Zhongnanhai. But in 1970 she was sent—perhaps on Mao's instructions—to one of the rectification institutions, known as "May 7 cadre schools," where hard agricultural labor was combined with ideological study. This particular "school" was in the Jinggangshan region, where Mao had led his guerrilla forces in 1928 and 1929. Now, in an odd echo of Mao's relationship there with He Zizhen, Li Na fell in love with one of the men who were supposed to be guarding her, and married him. The couple separated a few years afterward, but at the time of the separation Li Na was already pregnant, and she bore a child in 1973, providing Mao with his third grandson.

There is no logical way to date the ending of the Cultural Revolution. For many the height of its political fury was during 1966 and 1967, but in many of its aspects—the feuds between rival groups, the long years spent living with peasants in poor areas of the countryside, the fears of sudden raids on home and property, the insistent rhetoric against any aspect of the old society, the disruption of schools, and the management of most institutions through revolutionary committees—the extremist policies endured. The cultural sphere, where Jiang Qing had the strongest hold, was strictly regimented, and the content of art was intensely monitored until the mid-1970s. Also, the ongoing tensions in the country were exacerbated by the continuing bad relations with the Soviet Union. In 1969 these erupted into armed clashes along the northern Sino-Soviet border, leading to new mass-mobilization campaigns and the spread of war scares and a fresh hunt for traitors and "revisionists."

Mao was restless, and traveled widely during this period. Perhaps because he wished to get away from what he found was the oppressive atmosphere of Beijing, or to distance himself from Jiang Qing, he lived for long periods on his special train or in the various guest houses around the country that were always at his disposal. Though his health was not good and his eyesight was deteriorating rapidly, he seems to have kept up liaisons with various young companions.

Mao had always had irregular sleep patterns—he told friends that this was because his sleep naturally followed lunar phases, rather than the rhythms of the solar time to which most other people responded—and he took either Seconal or chloral hydrate for insomnia, getting the drugs through his physicians from a pharmacy where they were prepared for him under a code name. He also ate erratically and had poor teeth, which sometimes abscessed. In 1970, Mao had a serious case of pneumonia.

What seems to have weakened Mao's health far more than his irregular habits and wayward lifestyle was the extraordinary shock caused to him by the defection of Lin Biao in 1971. Though the details of exactly what occurred remain elusive, it seems that Lin Biao had come to suspect that Mao was losing faith in him, and that Mao hence had abandoned any idea of making Lin his revolutionary successor. In anger and desperation, Lin and some close army confidants conceived a plan to assassinate Mao by blowing up his train, and then to take over the government. When the plot was discovered on September 13, 1971, Lin fled from China in an air force plane, with several of his family members. The plane crashed in Mongolia, and all aboard were killed. It was the most bizarre of stories, with countless loose ends, but certainly Lin Biao was dead and Mao felt betrayed. After he received the news, Mao spent days lying in bed or shuffling around his room in Zhongnanhai. His insomnia worsened, his speech slurred, and his lower legs and feet swelled up. In January 1972 he was diagnosed as having congestive heart failure, and the swelling of his limbs had grown worse, extending to his neck.

This growing physical weakness coincided with the last internationally significant act in Mao's life: his decision to invite the president of the United States to China. Such a visit would be a first step toward repairing the diplomatic relations that had been severed since the outbreak of the Korean War in

1950, and that were now freeing up somewhat, since in August 1971 the United Nations had voted to give Taiwan's seat to the mainland regime, and the United States had not resisted. It would also lead to a realignment in global power, as the United States would be called in as a counterbalance to the Soviet Union, which Mao now saw as the greater threat. A détente with the United States might also hasten a settlement of the Vietnam War and prevent any further Soviet meddling there. It would also reassert Mao's own power as a major foreign-policy decision-maker.

The preliminary negotiations between Henry Kissinger and Zhou Enlai took place in complete secrecy during 1971, because so much was at stake for both sides. But on February 18, 1972, all preparations smoothly completed, President Richard Nixon and Henry Kissinger walked together into Mao's study in Zhongnanhai. The president noticed that Mao had to be helped to his feet by a "girl secretary," and his first words to Nixon were "I can't talk very well." During their informal conversation, moreover, Mao was self-deprecatory. Praised by the two Americans for the power of his political writings and his effect on the world, Mao replied that "there is nothing instructive in what I wrote" and that he had no effect on changing the world: "I've only been able to change a few places in the vicinity of Beijing." In a similar vein, when his own words that one should "seize the day" were quoted to him by the president, Mao responded, "I think that, generally speaking, people like me sound like a lot of big cannons." Such phrases, said Mao, had no more significance than things like "The whole world should unite and defeat imperialism, revisionism, and all reactionaries, and establish socialism." As they walked to the door, Mao was shuffling and said he had not been feeling well.

"You look very good," Nixon responded. "Appearances are deceiving," answered Mao. Kissinger, too, while noting Mao's strong grasp of international politics, and the wit and appropriateness of his responses, observed that Mao needed "two assistants' help" to rise from his armchair, and that Mao "could move only with difficulty and speak but with considerable effort." Mao's doctor mentioned later that because of physical weakness Mao "practiced sitting down and getting up" for days before his meeting with Nixon.

It had been an extraordinary shift in policy by Mao, to upend the strident attacks on United States imperialism that had flooded China's airwaves and newspapers for decades, and it is proof of the extraordinary power that Mao knew he had over his own people. But it is one of the last times we can see that power being utilized to the full.

The last important example was Mao's 1973 decision to allow the purged Deng Xiaoping to return to power. Deng had been ousted in the early years of the Cultural Revolution, but had never been mistreated as savagely as Liu Shaoqi or Peng Dehuai, and had spent the years of his disgrace living in Jiangxi and working—at least some of the time—in a tractor plant. Mao had even said that "if Lin Biao's health should fail him, I will let Xiaoping come back." Deng had laid the groundwork for his return by writing a correctly abject self-criticism, in which he admitted all the charges against him and announced that he would "sincerely and without any reservations accept the denunciations and accusations directed at me by the Party and the revolutionary masses." Deng expressed a willingness to die for his misdeeds, but added that his greatest hope would be to have "a trivial task of some sort that will provide me with an opportunity to make up for my past mistakes and to turn over a new leaf." Mao's 1973 order that Deng Xioaping be recalled for active duty in Beijing deepened the rift—already long-standing—between Mao and his wife, Jiang Qing, for she and Deng loathed each other. By 1973 Mao was open about his dislike and distrust of Jiang Qing, and it is possible that Mao's recall of Deng was done partly to infuriate her. Her attempt to stall Deng's return could have been the trigger for a harsh letter Mao wrote her in 1974, which contained the sentences: "It would be better for us not to see each other. For years I have advised you about many things, but you have ignored most of it. So what use is there for us to see each other?"

Though Mao's health had improved during 1973, and he seemed alert and even spritely at times, the debilitating symptoms that the Americans had noticed in 1972 were confirmed in July 1974 by medical tests that showed Mao had amyotrophic lateral sclerosis, the motor-neuron condition known as "Lou Gehrig's disease." By this time he was having great trouble reading, and sometimes eating and talking, since he could not fully close his mouth. Also, the muscles on the right side of his body began to atrophy. That fall and winter, Mao took extended trips in his special train, against his doctors' objections: one to Wuhan and one to Changsha, scene of so many of his youthful revolutionary activities. There he tried for a last time to swim, but it turned out to be impossible. He took mainly liquid food and spent much of the time lying in bed on his left side. Yet he still followed political events enough to stop a new attempt to prevent Deng's rise, for he knew that Zhou Enlai was dying of cancer and Deng would be the only major check to Jiang Qing and her inner circle. And Mao was able to sustain his end of the conversation when Kissinger returned to China with President Gerald Ford in 1975, even though Mao's words were mumbled and indistinct, and he often wrote out his responses on a pad of paper held by his nurse.

But in the main, Mao was restricted to following the political dramas through intermediaries. One of his contacts with the Politburo was his nephew Mao Yuanxin, whom Mao trusted, even though the young man was close to Jiang Qing. For those seeking to communicate with Mao himself, the main route was now through his female confidant and attendant Zhang Yufeng, who could transform his murmured sounds into intelligible words for others, and was the one who read many of the policy documents aloud to him. Fifty years younger than Mao, Zhang had been born in Manchuria in 1944 while it was still the puppet Japanese state of Manchukuo, and after finishing high school she got a job in 1960 serving on the trains used by senior cadres and foreign dignitaries. In 1962 she was assigned to Mao's private train, and by the end of that year, on a journey to Changsha, she became one of the young women who regularly joined Mao for dance parties. Although she had married a worker in the railway bureau in 1967, and bore him a daughter, Zhang Yufeng began to accompany Mao on all his long trips, including a three-month journey along the Yangtze in 1969. The following year she joined him as a personal attendant in his home in Zhongnanhai. They separated for a while, after an argument, but she was ordered to return. Thereafter she became Mao's secretary and nurse, and as his sight failed, she read key documents to him. From 1972 onward, the two of them regularly ate together, and she began to control access to Mao by deciding how and when his health made it suitable for visitors to be with him. She had become Mao's main conduit to the outside world.

A cataract operation in the summer of 1975 and the fitting

of special glasses gave Mao back some reading ability, and he was even able to watch movies with Zhang Yufeng in his study. Invited members of his staff were allowed to watch the same movies in a special screening room nearby. But Mao sometimes needed oxygen to breathe, and his right side was virtually paralyzed. His doctors decided, over his objections, to give him amino acids intravenously. When Zhou Enlai was dying of cancer in the hospital in January 1976, Mao was considered too ill to visit him. Through his nephew Mao Yuanxin, Mao did receive news of the great crowds that assembled to mourn the dead premier in Tiananmen Square on the tomb-sweeping day of April 5. Through the same source he heard of the swift and violent military and police suppression of the demonstration. Though Mao had previously backed Deng Xiaoping's return to power, he appears to have agreed with the argument made by some senior colleagues that Deng Xiaoping's scheming lay behind the demonstrations, and that Deng should be again dismissed. It seems to have been Mao's personal decision to appoint Hua Guofeng, formerly the Party secretary in Hunan province, to be the new premier, and Party first vice chairman. This remarkable promotion transformed the previously almost unknown Hua into Mao's probable successor. Though an odd and risky decision, the appointment of Hua was a deliberate compromise, to balance off Deng Xiaoping supporters against those of Jiang Qing.

Mao suffered a major heart attack on May 11, 1976, and the Politburo decided—without informing him—that they would choose on a case-by-case basis whether to share their deliberations with him. At the same time they began to hold some of their meetings in the swimming-pool area next to Mao's rooms, so they could be present swiftly in any emergency. On June 26,

Mao had a second heart attack. A third came on September 2, more serious than the previous two, leaving him weakened and comatose. On September 8, he was alert enough to spend some short periods reading reports, but he dozed off repeatedly. Around 11:15 P.M., he drifted into a coma. Ten minutes after midnight, on September 9, 1976, Mao died in the presence of the ranking members of the Politburo, who had been summoned to his room, and his attendant physicians.

The nearest thing that we have to Mao's thoughts about his approaching death comes from notes of a meeting he held, with several members of the Politburo, in Zhongnanhai on June 15, shortly before his second heart attack. Mao told his colleagues that reaching the age of seventy was unusual, and passing eighty inevitably made one think about funeral arrangements. It was therefore time to implement the old Chinese saying that, when appropriate, one should "seal the coffin and pass the final verdict." Mao had done two things that mattered, he said. He had battled Chiang Kai-shek for years and finally chased him off to "that little island" of Taiwan. And in the long war of resistance he had "asked the Japanese to return to their ancestral home" and had fought his way into the Forbidden City. Few people would argue that those were achievements. But what about the Cultural Revolution, where he had few supporters and "quite a few opponents"? That revolution remained unfinished, said Mao, and all he could do was pass the task on to the next generation. If he could not pass it on peacefully, then he would have to pass it on in turmoil. "What will happen to the next generation if it all fails?" he asked. "There may be a foul wind and a rain of blood. How will you cope? Heaven only knows!"

NOTES

The most important Western guide to the life and works of Mao Zedong is Stuart Schram, whose *The Political Thought of Mao Tse-tung* was published in 1963 (Paris and New York), and was soon followed by his closely researched biography, *Mao Tse-tung*, (New York, 1966). Over the last few years, Schram has been occupied with an immense project to assemble and translate all the works that can reasonably and reliably be attributed to Mao, under the general title *Mao's Road to Power: Revolutionary Writings, 1912–1949*. To date, four volumes have appeared, all published by M. E. Sharpe, Armonk, N.Y.: vol. 1, *The Pre-Marxist Period, 1912–1920* (1992); vol. 2, *National Revolution and Social Revolution, December 1920–June 1927* (1994); vol. 3, *From the Jinggangshan to the Establishment of the Jiangxi Soviets, July 1927–December 1930* (1995); and vol. 4, *The Rise and Fall of the Chinese Soviet Republic, 1931–1934* (1997). Many intriguing details, though one needs to sift through them with care, were provided by Mao himself in his celebrated 1936 interview with Edgar Snow, conducted after the Long March and published by Snow to great acclaim as *Red Star Over China* (New York, 1938). Another useful earlier study was Jerome Ch'en, *Mao and the Chinese Revolution* (Oxford, 1965). A lively biography, based on wide reading but also with much reconstructed dialogue, is Ross Terrill, *Mao: A Biography* (New York, 1980, and subsequent revisions). In 1993 a group of scholars in China, under the general editor Pang Xianzhi, compiled a detailed chronological biography of Mao, *Mao Zedong nianpu, 1893–1949*, 3 vols. (Beijing, 1993). Another immensely useful translation containing many of Mao's personal letters, is Michael Y. M. Kau and John K. Leung, eds., *The Writings of Mao Zedong, 1949–1976*, of which two volumes have appeared to date: vol.1, *September 1949–December 1955* (Armonk, N.Y., 1986), and vol. 2, *January 1956–December 1957* (Armonk, N.Y., 1992). Scores of volumes of reminiscences and anecdotes about Mao, and of memoirs by those who worked for him, have been appearing in China in recent years. Some are referred to below.

Chapter 1

Mao's account of his childhood to Snow in *Red Star Over China*, especially pp. 122–34, remains a basic source. Other invaluable backup sources from Mao's early letters and writings are in Stuart Schram, *Mao's Road to Power*, vol. 1, *The Pre-Marxist Period, 1912–1920*. Here, I draw especially on pp. 59–65 for two 1915 letters by Mao to friends, and for a reminiscence from his teacher, and on pp. 419–20 for Mao's euology at his mother's funeral. Details on the Luo family and Mao's first wife are given by Xiao Feng, in *Mao Zedong zhimi* (Beijing, 1992), pp. 128–29. On the 1911 revolution and the events in Hunan, admirable background books are Mary C. Wright, *China in Revolution: The First Phase* (New Haven, 1968), and Joseph Esherick, *Reform and Revolution in China: The 1911 Revolution in Hunan and Hubei* (Berkeley, 1976), especially pp. 155–58 and 204–10 on Jiao and Chen.

Chapter 2

On Mao's formative school years, the information Mao gave to Snow in *Red Star Over China*, especially on pp. 139–50, can now be supplemented with a mass of newly available Chinese material, translated in Schram, *Mao's Road to Power*. These include Mao's earliest surviving schoolboy essay on Lord Shang (vol. 1, pp. 5–6), his 1913 reading notes on classical Chinese texts (vol. 1, pp. 40–43), a friend's account of their outings and swims (vol. 1, pp. 137–40), and the complete run of Paulsen study notes (vol. 1, pp. 175–310). The Hunan study-group meetings and Ms. Tao's comments are in Schram, vol. 2, especially pp. 18–19, 25, and 80–85.

Chapter 3

A detailed study of Hunan in this period of Mao's life is Angus W. McDonald, *The Urban Origins of Rural Revolution: Elites and the Masses in Hunan Province, China, 1911–1927* (Berkeley, 1978). The best study about "The May Fourth Movement" is still Chow Tse-tsung, *The May Fourth Movement, Intellectual Revolution in Modern China*, (Cambridge, Mass., 1960). Schram, *Mao's Road to Power*, vol. 1, has key material on Mao's mother's illness (p. 317), the July 1919 manifesto (pp. 319–20), the critique of General Zhang (pp. 476–86), Mao's Russian- and English-language forays (p. 518), and the Cultural Book Society (pp. 534–35). Schram, ibid., vol. 2, pp. 56–58, has the bookshop investors' list. In Snow, *Red Star Over China*, the main details for Mao at this stage of his life are on pp. 148–51. Andrew Nathan, *Peking Politics, 1918–1923: Factionalism and the Failure of Constitutionalism* (New York, 1976), bravely tackles the tangled politics of the capital at this time.

Chapter 4

For the detailed background history of the early Communist Party, an essential work is Tony Saich, *The Rise to Power of the Chinese Communist Party* (Armonk, N.Y., 1996), which gives the full texts of the documents mentioned here, and careful background on the First Congress. The same author's *The Origins of the First United Front in China: The Role of Sneevliet (alias Maring)*, 2 vols. (Leiden, 1991), gives meticulous details on the early Comintern in China. About the Chinese in France, many of them Mao's friends from Changsha, the finest source is Marilyn A. Levine, *The Found*

Generation: Chinese Communists in Europe During the Twenties (Seattle, 1993). Mao's early strike activities are well covered in Lynda Shaffer, *Mao and the Workers: The Hunan Labor Movement, 1920–1923* (Armonk, N.Y., 1982). For the details from Mao's correspondence, see Schram, *Mao's Road to Power*, vol.1, pp. 546–47, on the references to Lenin, and pp. 608–9 for the references to marriage and rape. The bookshop expansion is in ibid., vol. 2, pp. 46–53; the letters to France on Marxism are in vol. 2, pp. 7–8; the New People's Study Society is explored in vol. 2, pp. 28–32 and pp. 68–70; and the Confucian Academy as a front in vol. 2, pp. 89–96.

Chapter 5

The basic source on the Hunan strikes is Shaffer, *Mao and the Workers*, which details the work of the returned students Liu Shaoqi (from Moscow) and Li Lisan (from France) in the mining strikes at the Anyuan collieries and railyards, and the Shuikoushan lead and zinc mines; she covers Mao and the carpenters on pp. 119–42, and Mao and the printers on pp. 148–61. Saich, *Rise to Power*, gives full documentation for Chen Duxiu's negative views on the United Front, Chen's 1923 Party figures, and Mao's 1923 description of Hunan's problems. Snow, *Red Star Over China*, p. 159, gives Mao's statement on the missed 1922 Party Congress. Schram, *Mao's Road to Power*, vol. 2, has Mao's 1923 strike tables (pp. 172–77), the report of his 1926 Changsha speech (pp. 420–22), the 1926 Xiangtan report (pp. 478–83), and the entire Hunan report of 1927 (pp. 429–68). The Hunan tables are on p. 442, and the cited passage is on p. 430. The cited passage from the Great Union of the Popular Masses is from Schram, vol. 1, p. 386. The Chinese transcript of the original version of Mao's poem of 1923 to Yang Kaihui is given in Xiao Yongyi, ed., *Mao Zedong shici duilian jizhu* (Changsha, 1991), pp. 10–13; I have used this version, and especially the original closing four lines of the poem as given there, to amend the translation of the revised later version of the poem in Schram, vol. 2, pp. 195–96.

NOTES

Chapter 6

The basic documentary history of the period is given in Saich, *Rise to Power*. A powerful earlier account of the events of 1927 is Harold Isaacs, *The Tragedy of the Chinese Revolution* (Stanford, 1961), which can be supplemented with Jean Chesneaux, *The Chinese Labor Movement, 1919–1927* (Stanford, 1968), and with Elizabeth Perry, *Shanghai on Strike: The Politics of Chinese Labor* (Stanford, 1993). The period after 1928 is covered in S. Bernard Thomas, *Labor and the Chinese Revolution* (Ann Arbor, 1983). Mao's 1927 writings on the need for grasping the barrel of the gun are given in Schram, *Mao's Road to Power*, vol. 3, pp. 21–31 and 35–36, his Changsha campaign dreams in vol. 3, p. 44. The Jinggangshan material is in Schram, vol. 3, pp. 51–130. Schram, vol. 3, pp. 192–93, gives the text about Yang Kaihui in Mao's letter to Li Lisan. Yang Kaihui's October 1928 poem for Mao is printed in Xiao Yongyi, ed., *Mao Zedong shici*, pp. 99–100.

Details on the birth of Mao and Yang's third child, Anlong, and the various children born to Mao and He Zizhen, are discussed in Bin Zi, *Mao Zedong de ganqing shijie* (Jilin, 1990), pp. 32, 95, and 124–30, and in Ye Yonglie, *Jiang Qing zhuan* (Beijing, 1993), pp. 163–68. The subsequent fates of Anlong, Anying, and Anqing are given in Xiu Juan, *Mao Zedong Yuqin zhuan* (Beijing, 1993), pp. 42–43 and 83–84. The text of Mao's entire Jiangxi investigation is translated and analyzed by Roger Thompson, *Mao Zedong: Report from Xunwu* (Stanford, 1990). The politics of the Long March and the Zunyi meetings are studied in detail by Benjamin Yang, *From Revolution to Politics: Chinese Communists on the Long March* (Boulder, 1990). Edgar Snow noted the birth of Mao and He's daughter Li Min in *Red Star Over China*, p. 72.

Chapter 7

The texts of the main Xian discussions and Yan'an political debates can be found in Saich, *Rise to Power*, pp. 769–87, and the protest made by Wang Shiwei against Mao in ibid., p. 1107. The Yan'an talks are translated and explicated in Bonnie S. McDougall, *Mao Zedong's "Talks at the Yan'an Conference on Literature and Art"* (Ann Arbor, 1980). The various policies in the northern Communist base areas are finely analyzed in Pauline B. Keating, *Two Revolutions: Village Reconstruction and the Cooperative Movement in Northern Shaanxi, 1934–1945* (Stanford, 1997). The most thorough review of the growth of the Mao cult is that by Raymond F. Wylie, *The Emergence of Maoism: Mao Tse-tung, Ch'en Po-ta, and the Search for Chinese Theory, 1935–1945* (Stanford, 1980). Snow's *Red Star Over China* nicely depicts Mao's carefully honed self-presentation at this time. Chen Yung-fa, *Making Revolution: The Communist Movement in Eastern and Central China, 1937–1945* (Berkeley, 1986), shows the realities of life in the other main border areas. Gregor Benton, *Mountain Fires: The Red Army's Three-Year War in South China, 1934–1938* (Berkeley, 1992), explores the lives of those Communists left behind at the time of the Long March.

Chapter 8

Rather surprisingly, there is still no definitive book on the 1945–1949 civil war in China. The policies of the Soviet Union during the war are summarized in James Reardon-Anderson, *Yenan and the Great Powers: The Origins of Chinese Communist Foreign Policy, 1944–1946* (New York, 1980). Saich, *Rise to Power*, again gives the key Communist policy documents. The buildup of the Communists' base in Manchuria is explored by Steven Levine in *Anvil of Victory: The Communist Revolution in Manchuria, 1945–1948* (New York, 1987). The Mao-Stalin talks have been published in the *Bulletin of the Cold War International History Project*, issues 6 and 7, "The Cold War in Asia," Washington, D.C., winter 1995/1996, pp. 5–9. The possibilities of preserving Beijing and its walls as an ideal park-like city were pushed by Liang Sicheng, son of Mao's erstwhile reformist hero Liang Qichao. See Wilma Fairbank, *Liang and Lin: Partners in Exploring China's Architectural Past* (Philadelphia, 1994). Two important reevaluations of the Korean War, using many newly available Chinese sources, are Chen Jian, *China's Road to the Korean War: The Making of the Sino-American Confrontation* (New York, 1994), and Shu Guang Zhang, *Mao's Military Romanticism: China and the Korean War, 1950–1953*, (Lawrence, Kan., 1995). Mao's comments on the death of his son in Korea are given in Michael Kau and John Leung, eds., *The Writings of Mao Zedong, 1949–1976*, 2 vols. (Armonk, N.Y., 1986 and 1992), vol. 1, pp. 147–48.

Chapter 9

The personal letters to Mao cited here can be found in Kau and Leung, *The Writings of Mao Zedong*, vol. 1, pp. 13–14, 74–77, 233, and 448, on the Yang family: vol. 1, pp. 121–22 and 141 on former teachers; and vol. 1, pp. 36, 70, and 161 on local abuses. A careful analysis of the roles of Mao's confidential secretaries is in Dong Bian, ed., *Mao Zedong he tade mishu Tian Jiaying* (Beijing, 1989). Background documents on Mao's rural reforms are given in *Selected Works of Mao Tsetung*, vol. 5 (Peking, 1977), especially pp. 184–90 and 198–99. The important original draft of the February 1957 "Contradictions" speech is translated in full in Roderick MacFarquhar, Timothy Cheek, and Eugene Wu, eds., *The Secret Speeches of Chairman Mao: From the Hundred Flowers to the Great Leap Forward* (Cambridge, Mass., 1989), pp. 131–89. The 1957 Beidaihe talks are in ibid., pp. 397–441. On the early purges, see Frederick C. Teiwes, *Politics at Mao's Court, Gao Gang and Party Factionalism in the Early 1950s* (Armonk, N.Y., 1990). A useful overview of data and sources on the 1950s is Timothy Cheek and Tony Saich, eds., *New Perspectives on State Socialism in China* (Armonk, N.Y., 1997).

Chapter 10

Several new personal details on Mao's children and their spouses were released in *Beijing Review*, December 13, 1993, pp. 20–22, and on Jiang Qing and Mao in Ye Yonglie, *Jiang Qing zhuan*,

p. 240. On p. 248, Ye Yonglie gives details on He Zizhen in the 1950s. Mao's village talks are given in Leung and Kau, vol. 2, pp. 80, 83, and 299. His letter to spare the nanny Chen Yuying from labor duty is in Kau and Leung, *The Writings of Mao Zedong*, vol. 2, p. 803. Mao's poem for Yang Kaihui and Li Shuyi's husband was written on May 11, 1957, published the following New Year's Day in Hunan, and then later run in the national press. I follow the Chinese text and notes in Xiao Yongyi, *Mao Zedong shici*, pp. 96–99; in the translation I draw on the versions in Kau and Leung, vol. 2, p. 539, and in Ch'en, *Mao and the Chinese Revolution*, pp. 347–48. Deng Tuo's life is carefully evaluated in Timothy Cheek, *Propaganda and Culture in Mao's China: Deng Tuo and the Intelligentsia* (Oxford, England, 1997), especially pp. 178–81, for their crucial confrontation. An excellent source on the Lushan Plenum and Peng's role is Roderick MacFarquhar, *The Origins of the Cultural Revolution*, vol. 2, "The Great Leap Forward, 1958–1960" (New York, 1983), pp. 187–251; quotations are from pp. 197, 203, 247, and 249. For Mao's Great Leap poem from the Shaoshan visit of June 25, 1959, see Xiao Yongyi, pp. 106–8, and the English versions in Schram, *Mao Tse-tung*, p. 298, and Ch'en, p. 350.

Chapter 11

The investigative tours coordinated by Tian Jiaying are carefully explored in MacFarquhar, *The Origins of the Cultural Revolution* (New York, 1997), vol. 3, "The Coming of the Cataclysm, 1961–1966," especially pp. 39–43, 50–55, and 264–66. The suicides of Deng and Tian are discussed on pp. 456–60. The same book gives a detailed analysis of the various factional groupings and their policies prior to the Cultural Revolution, and is a good way to cross-check some of the most controversial parts of Li Zhisui's memoir, *The Private Life of Chairman Mao* (New York, 1994). Transcripts of Mao's talks with his nephew Mao Yuanxin are given in Stuart Schram, ed., *Chairman Mao Talks to the People: Talks and Letters*,

1956–1971 (New York, 1974), pp. 243–52. Mao's remark on the intellectuals cocking their tails is in Kau and Leung, *The Writings of Mao Zedong*, vol. 2, p. 611. The essay by Michael Schoenhals, "The Central Case Examination Group, 1966–79," *China Quarterly*, vol. 145, March 1996, pp. 87–111, examines that crucial organization. Schoenhals has also edited an invaluable collection of materials on the Cultural Revolution, *China's Cultural Revolution, 1966–1969: Not a Dinner Party* (Armonk, N.Y., 1996). See pp. 212–22 for the Number 26 Middle School manifesto. The most complex and powerful account of the turbulent emotions aroused in the young Red Guards that I have read is Rae Yang, *Spider Eaters: A Memoir* (Berkeley, 1997).

Chapter 12

Besides the informal documents in Schram, *Chairman Mao Talks to the People* (pp. 270–74), a useful collection of Mao's Cultural Revolution reflections is Jerome Ch'en, *Mao Papers, Anthology and Bibliography* (Oxford, England, 1970), quotations from pp. 35–36, 45–49, and 153. Mao Yuanxin's activities are mentioned in Li Zhisui, *The Private Life of Chairman Mao*, pp. 504–5, and Mao's harsh 1974 letter to Jiang Qing on p. 578. Li Zhisui mentions Li Na as a link with the students in pp. 468–69 and 504. Her Jinggangshan romance and pregnancy is discussed in Ye Yonglie, *Jiang Qing zhuan*, pp. 607–8. Li Zhisui's details of Mao's debilities seem to have been often exaggerated; a more vigorous and alert Mao comes across from the transcripts of Henry Kissinger's five visits with Mao between 1972 and 1975: see William Burr, ed., *The Kissinger Transcripts: The Top Secret Talks with Beijing and Moscow* (New York, 1999). Some of these materials are also in Richard Nixon, *RN, Memoirs* (New York, 1978), pp. 560–64, Henry Kissinger, *White House Years* (Boston, 1979), p. 1059, and Henry Kissinger, *Years of Renewal* (New York, 1999), pp. 868–99. Ruan Jihong collected valuable interview materials with Zhang Yufu, Mao's female attendant in his last years; they are published in

Huang Haizhou, ed., *Mao Zedong yishi* (Hunan, 1989), pp. 26–39. The medical reports of Mao's last hours are in Lin Ke et al., eds., *Lishi de zhenshi* (Hong Kong, 1995), pp. 190–98. On Mao's death thoughts, see Schoenhals, *China's Cultural Revolution*, p. 293.

Treason by the Book

Shortly before noon on October 28, 1728, General Yue Zhongqi, the most powerful military and civilian official in northwest China, was en route to his headquarters. Suddenly, out of the crowd, a stranger ran toward Yue and passed him an envelope containing details of a treasonous plot to overthrow the Manchu government. In this thrilling story of a conspiracy against the Qing dynasty, Spence has created a vivid portrait of the rich culture that surrounds one of the most dramatic moments in Chinese history.   *ISBN 0-14-200041-8*

The Memory Palace of Matteo Ricci

In 1577, the Jesuit priest Matteo Ricci set out from Italy to bring Christian faith and Western thought to Ming dynasty China. To capture the complex emotional and religious drama of Ricci's extraordinary life, Spence relates his subject's experiences with several images that Ricci himself created: four images derived from the events in the Bible and others from a book on the art of memory that Ricci wrote in Chinese and circulated among members of the Ming dynasty elite. A rich and compelling narrative about a remarkable life, *The Memory Palace of Matteo Ricci* is also a significant work of global history, juxtaposing the world of Counter-Reformation Europe with that of Ming China.   *ISBN 0-14-008098-8*

The Gate of Heavenly Peace
The Chinese and Their Revolution, 1895–1980

In this masterful, highly original approach to modern Chinese history, Jonathan D. Spence shows us the Chinese revolution through the eyes of its most articulate participants: the writers, historians, philosophers, and insurrectionists who shaped and were shaped by the turbulent events of this century. By skillfully combining literary materials with more conventional sources of political and social history, Spence provides an unparalleled look at China and her people and offers valuable insight into the continuing conflict between the implacable power of the state and the strivings of China's artists, writers, and thinkers.

ISBN 0-14-006279-3

To Change China
Western Advisers in China 1620–1960

"To change China" was the goal of foreign missionaries, soldiers, doctors, teachers, engineers, and revolutionaries for more than three hundred years. But the Chinese, while eagerly accepting Western technical advice, clung steadfastly to their own religious and cultural traditions. As a new era of relations between China and the United States begins, the tales in this volume will serve as cautionary histories for businessmen, diplomats, students, or any other foreigners who foolishly believe that they can transform this vast, enigmatic country.

ISBN 0-14-005528-2

The Death of Woman Wang

Award-winning author Jonathan D. Spence paints a vivid picture of an obscure place and time: provincial China in the seventeenth century. Life in the northeastern county of T'an-ch'eng emerges here as an endless cycle of floods, plagues, crop failures, banditry, and heavy taxation. Against this turbulent background a tenacious tax collector, an irascible farmer, and an unhappy wife act out a poignant drama at whose climax the wife, having run away from her husband, returns to him, only to die at his hands. Magnificently evoking the China of long ago, *The Death of Woman Wang* also deepens our understanding of the China we know today.   ISBN 0-14-005121-X